This Book Belongs To:

Alphabet
TRACE THE LETTERS

Tracing the letters

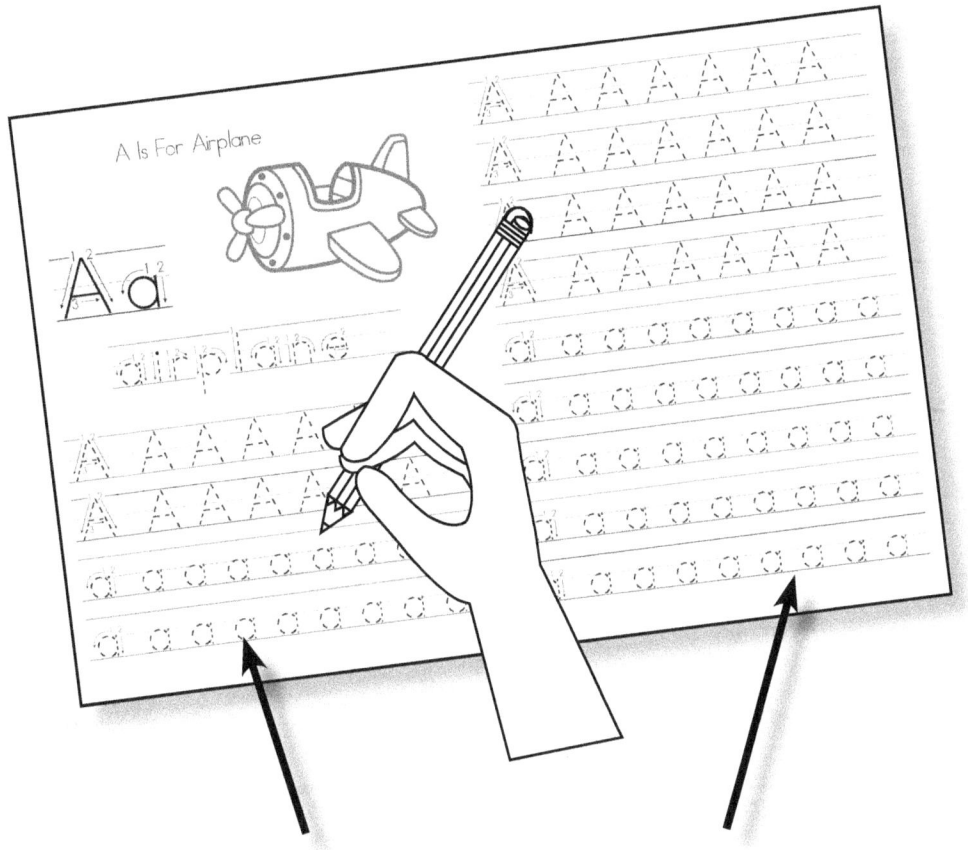

Follow the gray lines to
from the letters

A Is For Airplane

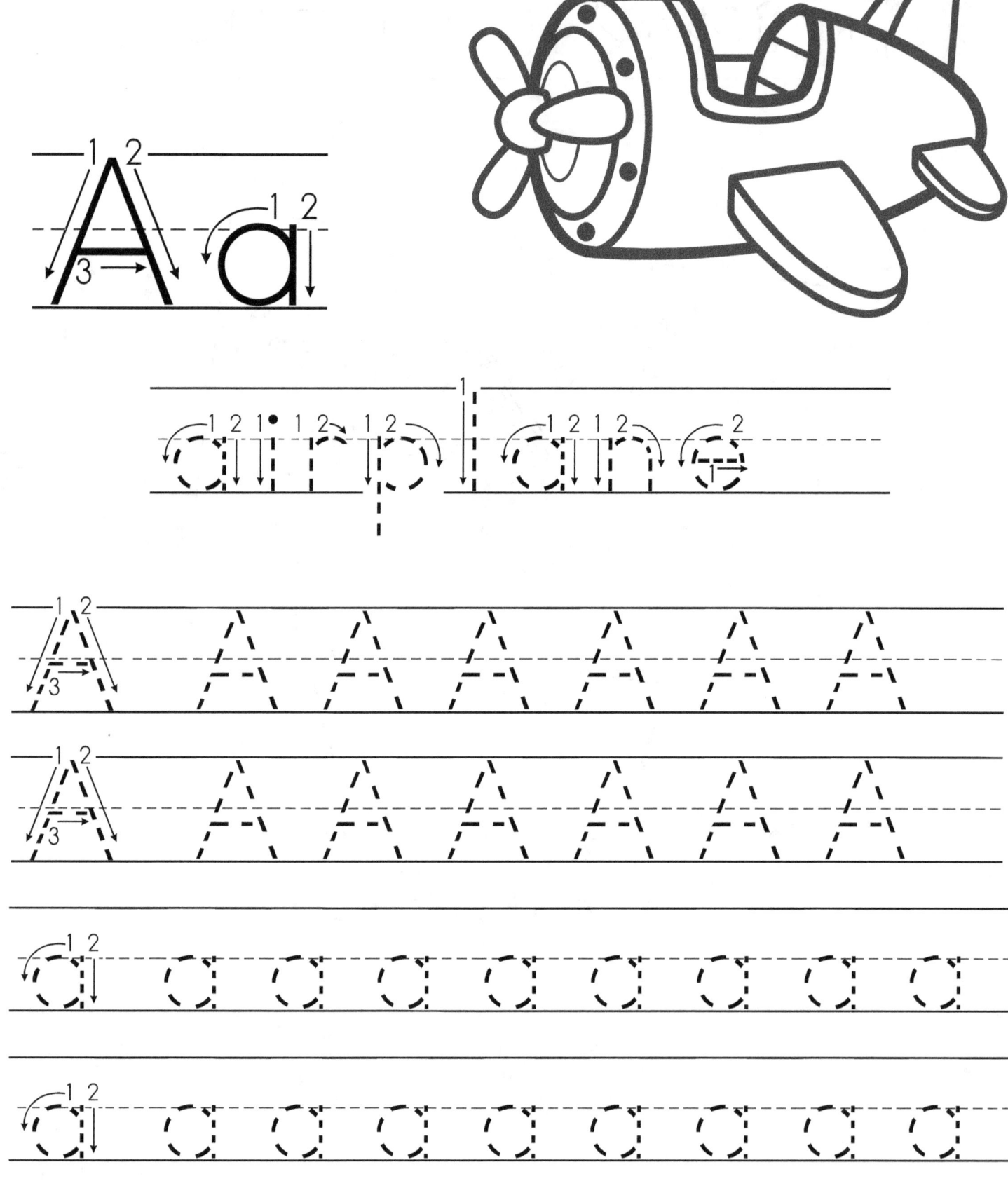

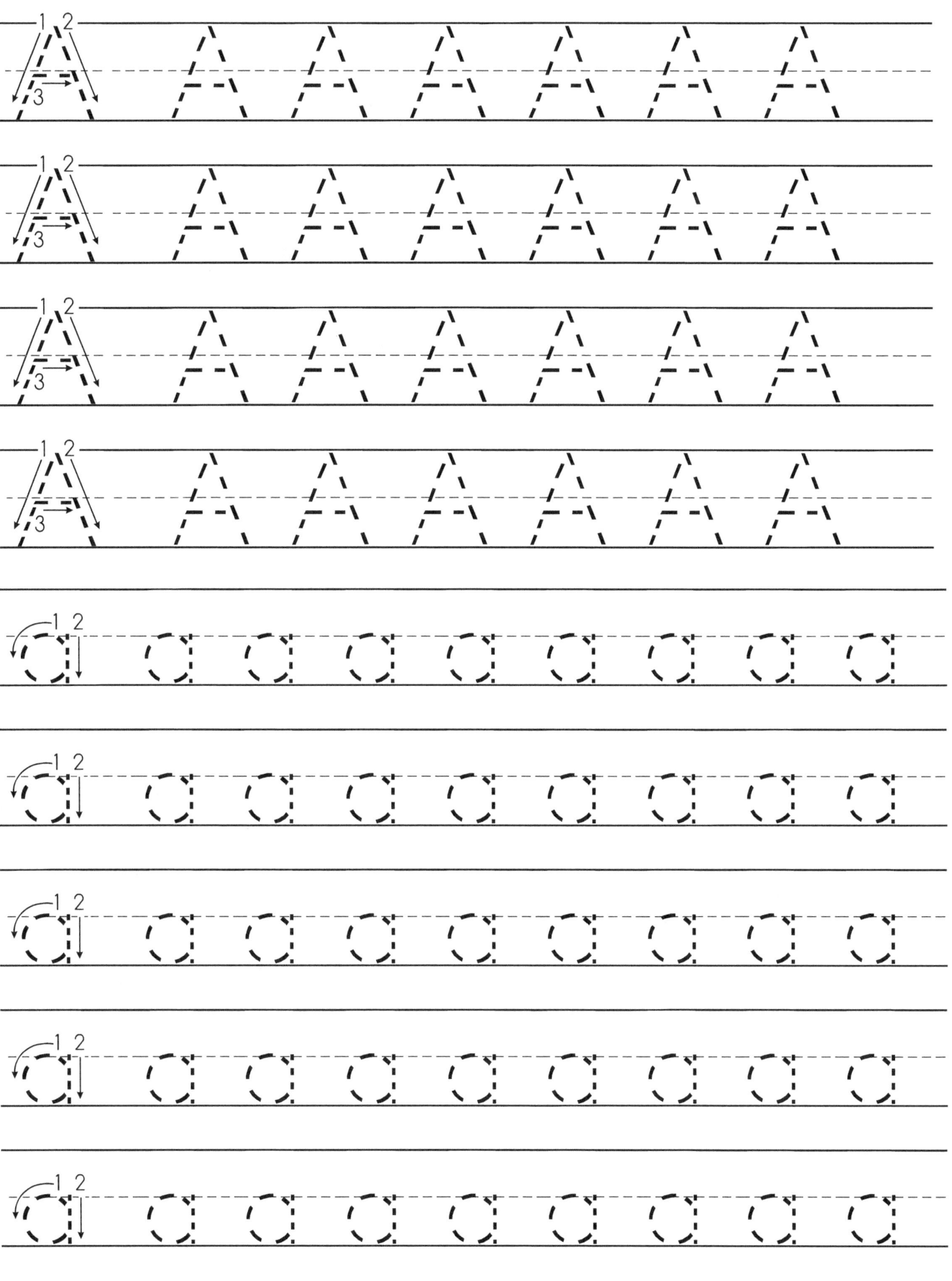

B Is For Ballon

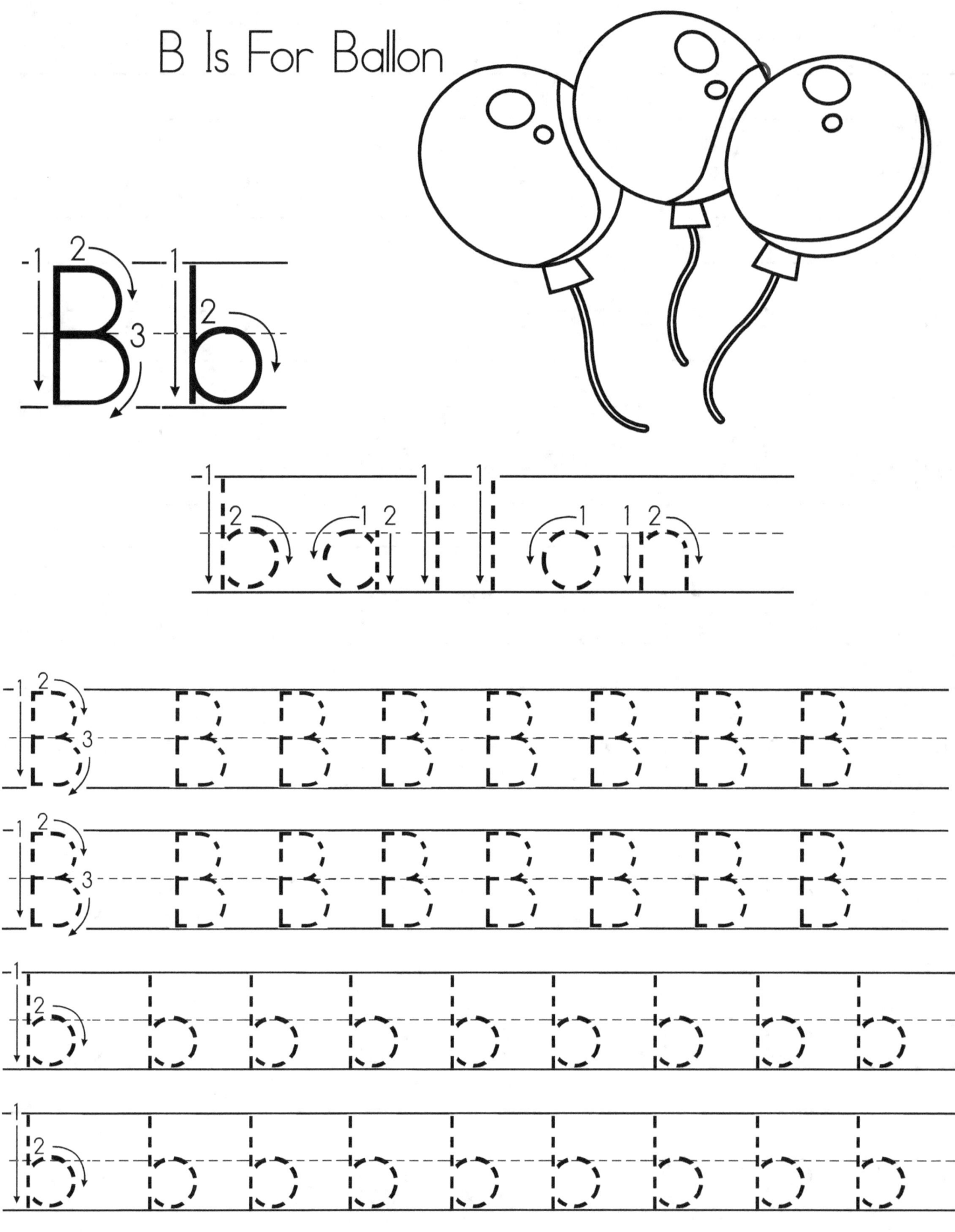

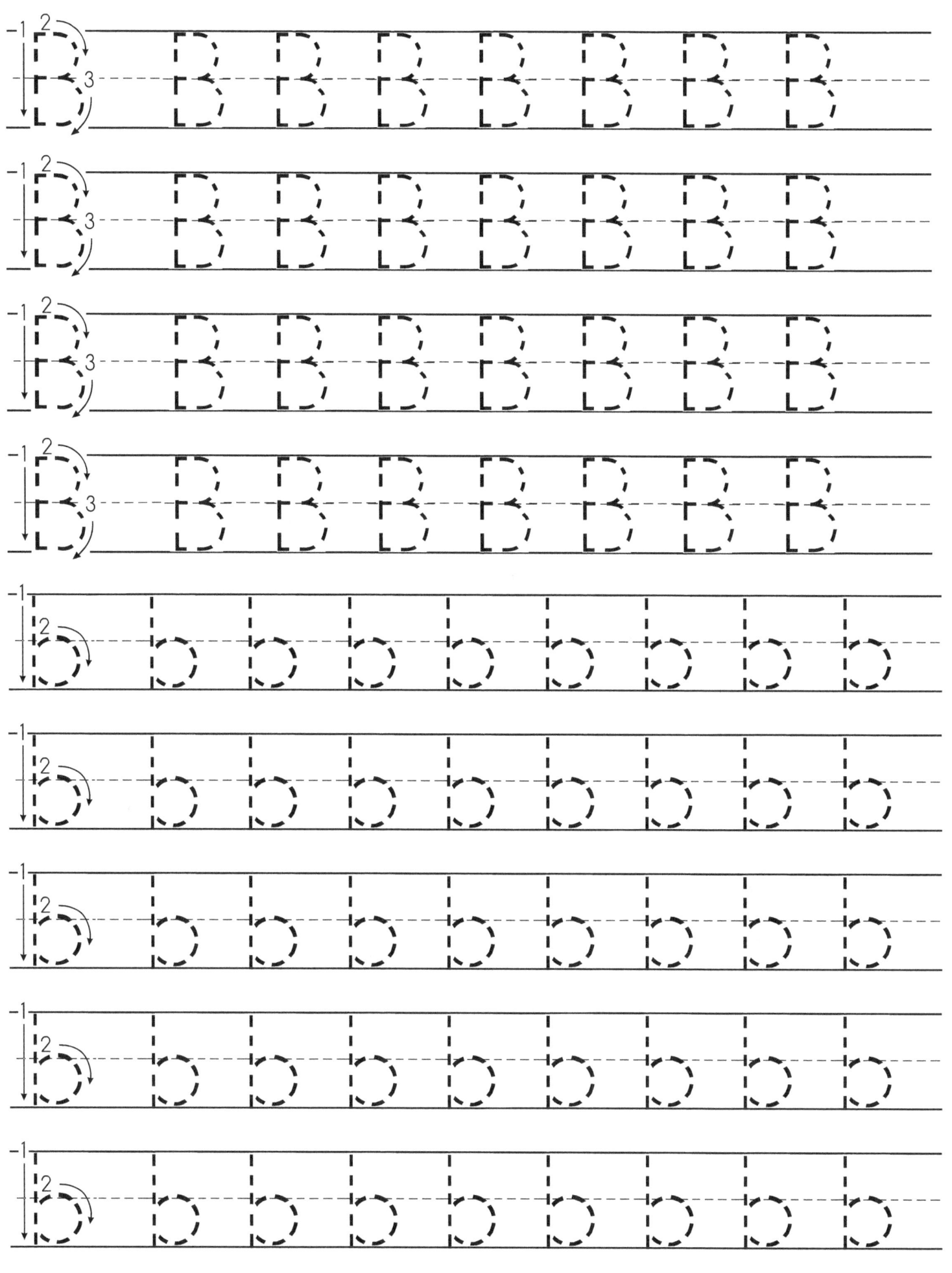

B Is For Cake

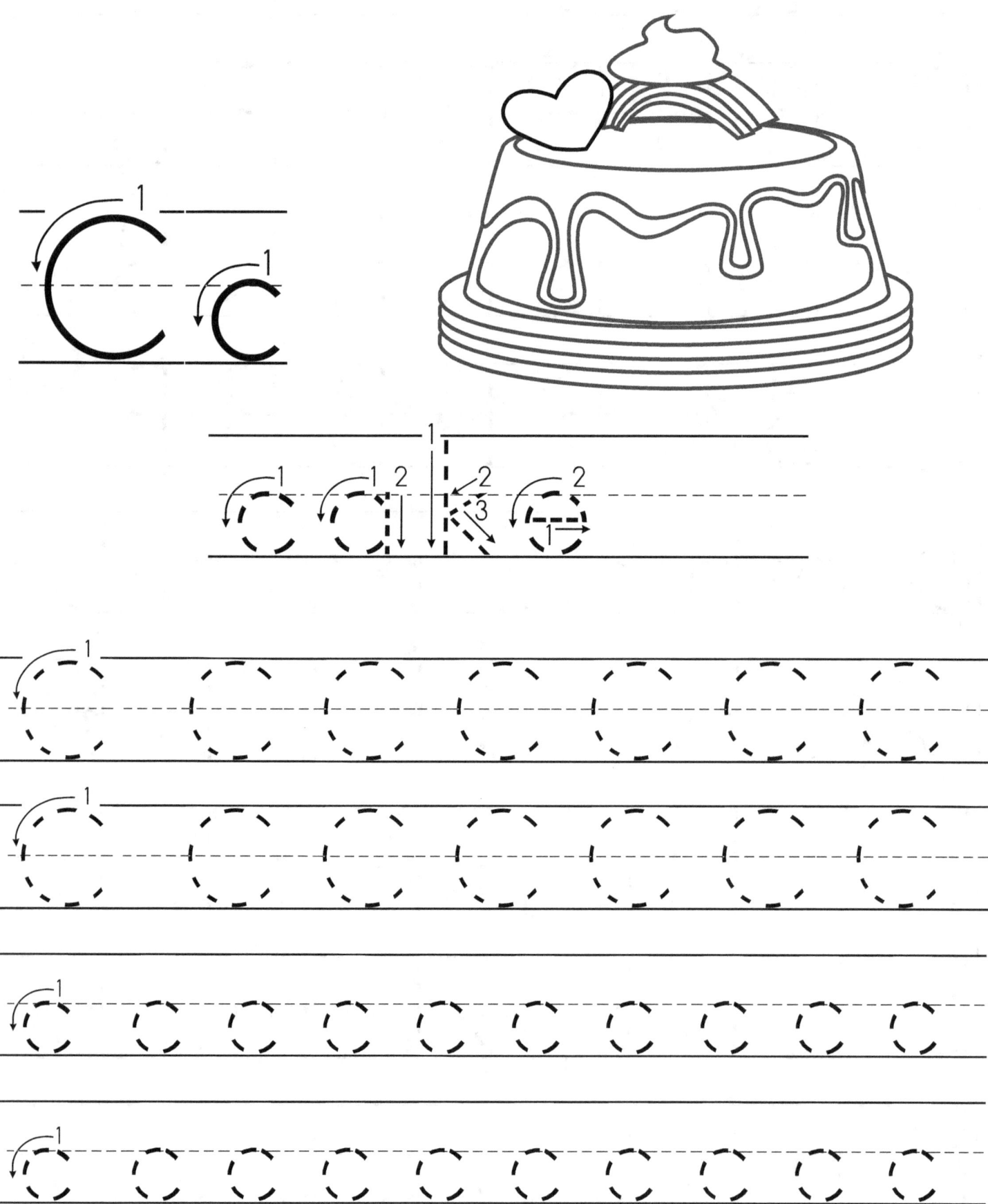

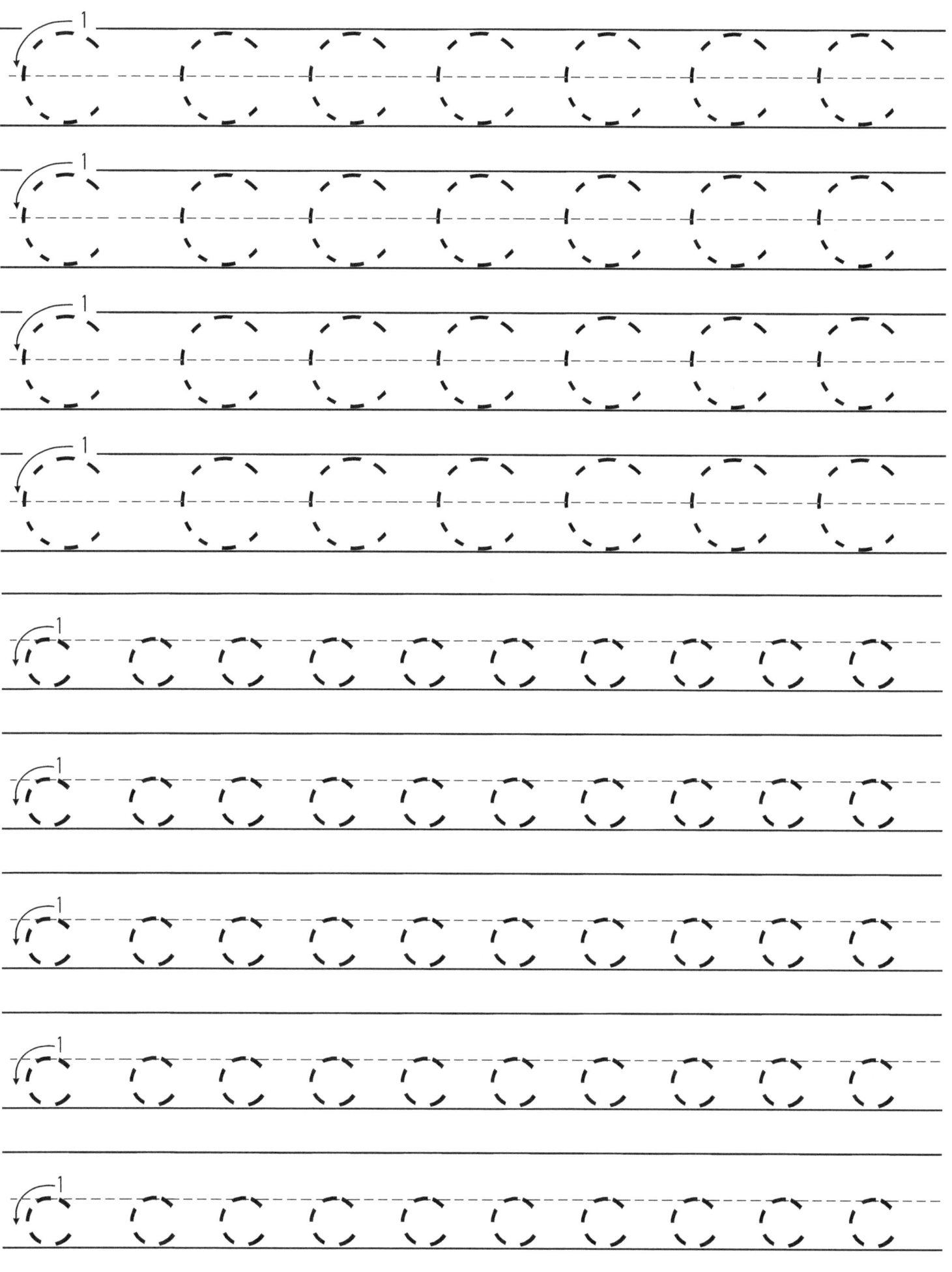

D Is For Drum

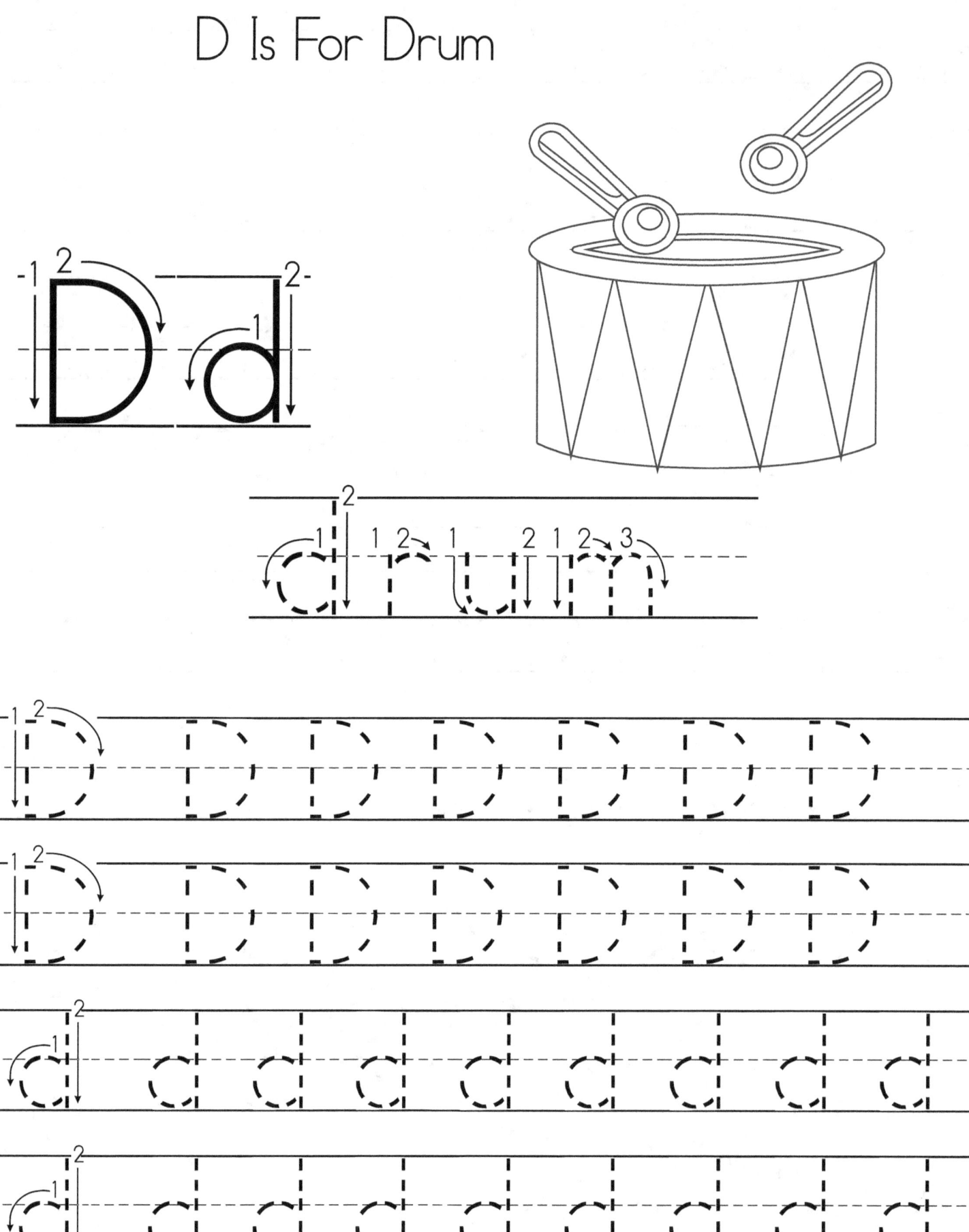

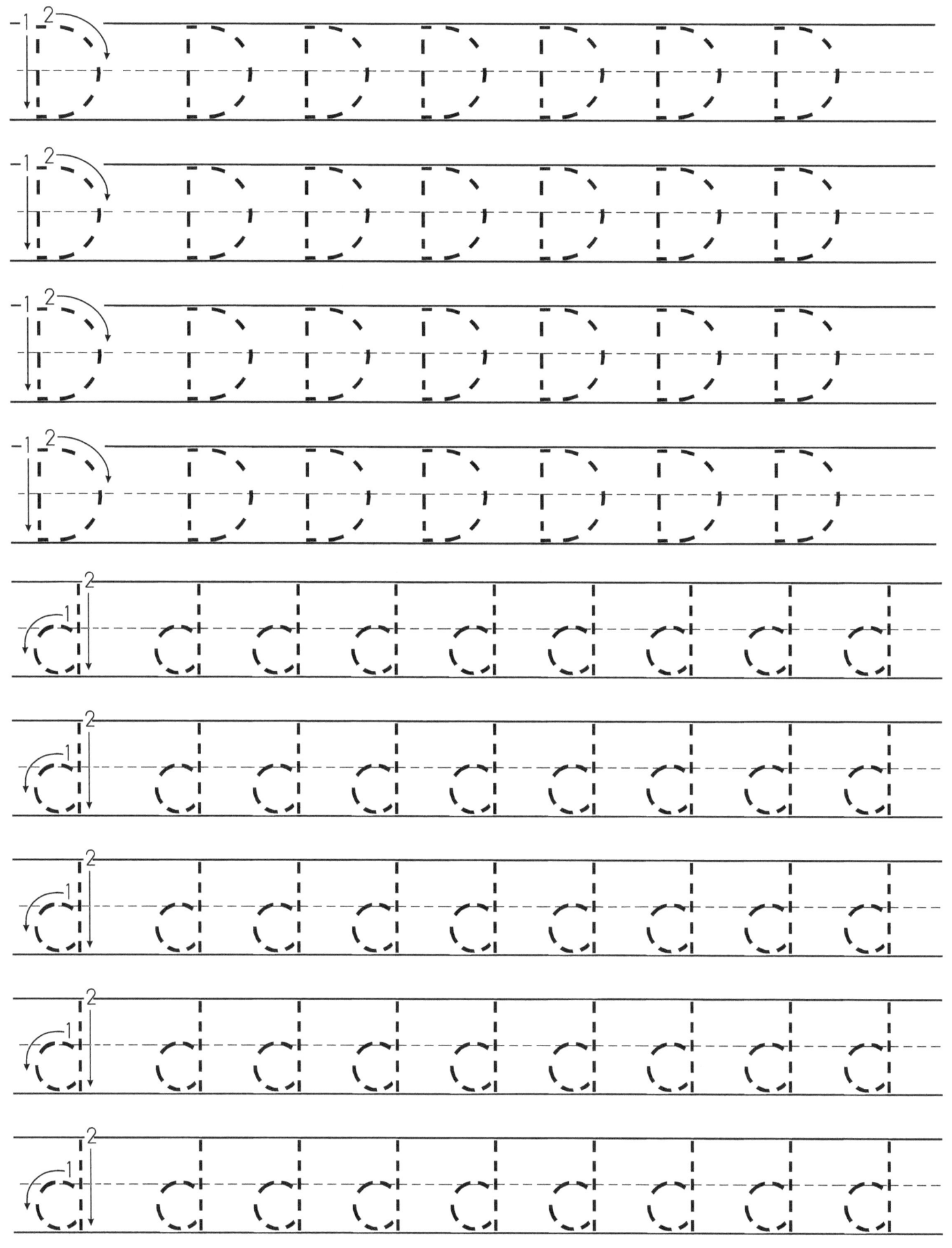

E Is For Earth

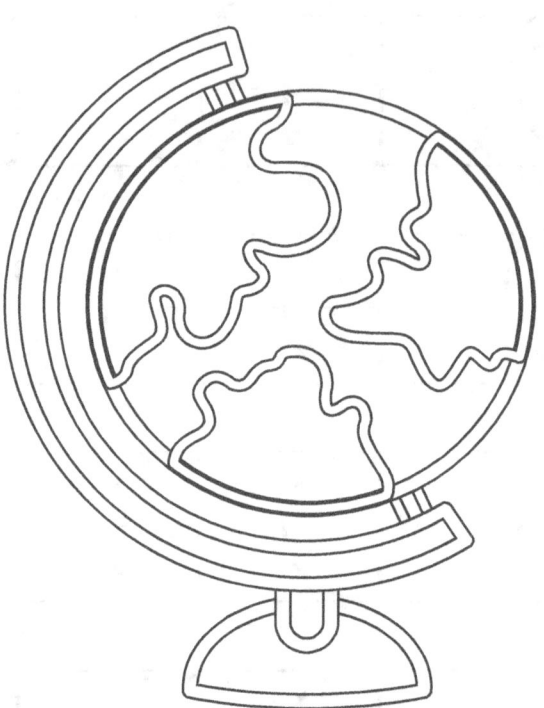

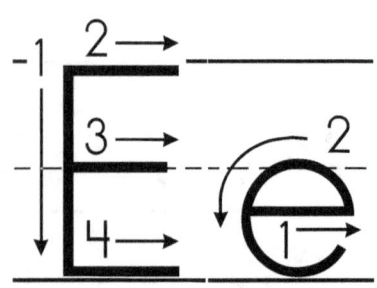

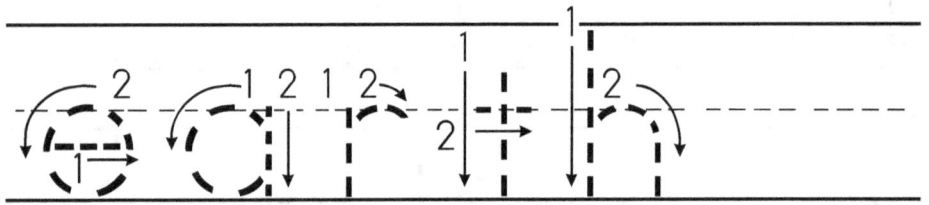

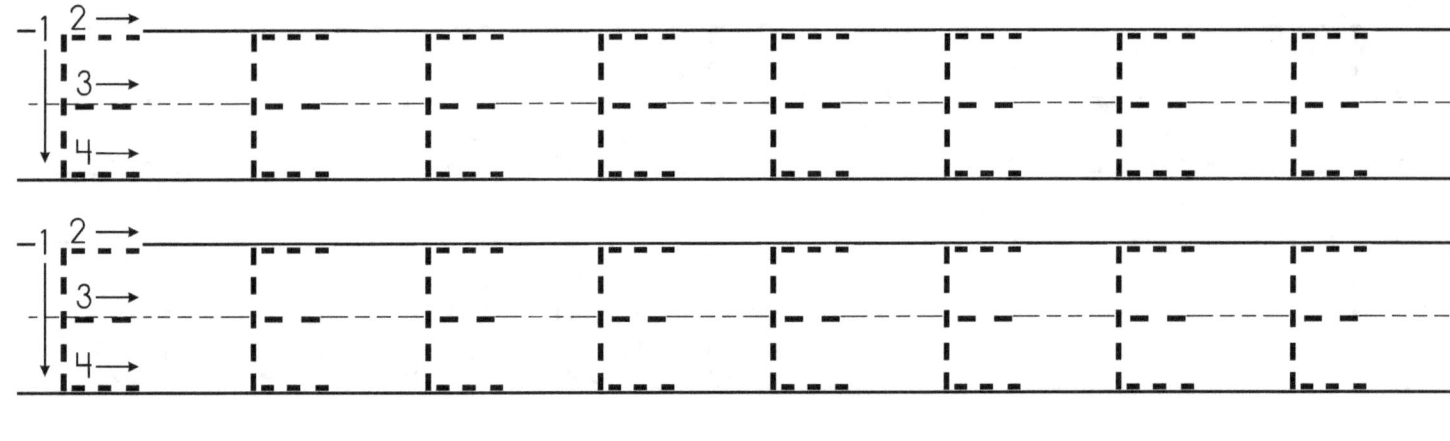

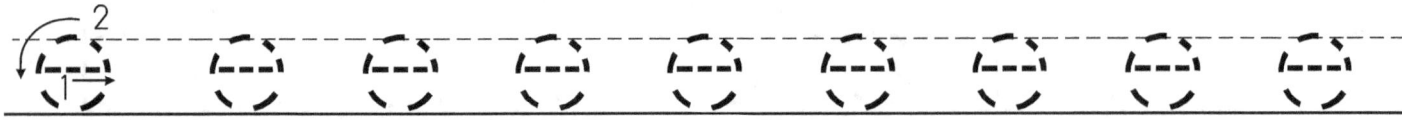

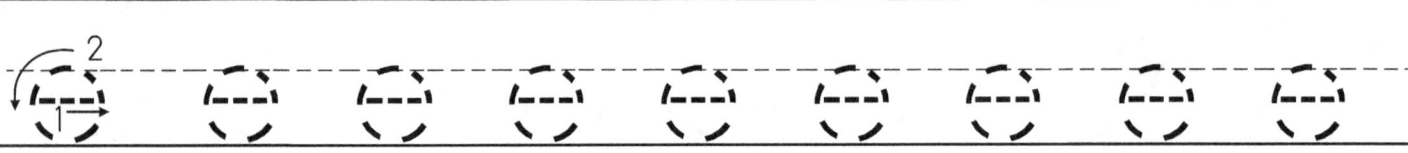

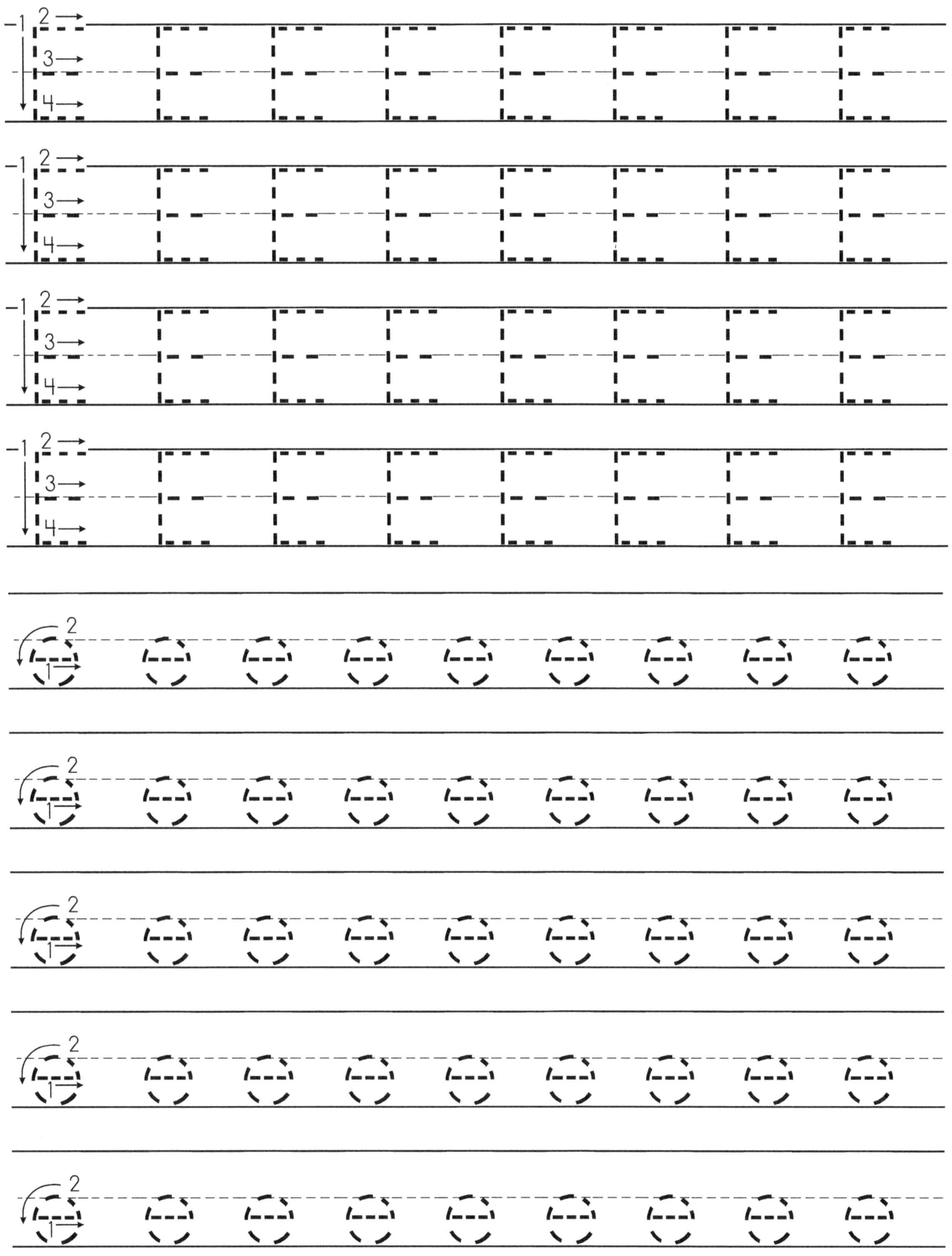

F Is For Fork

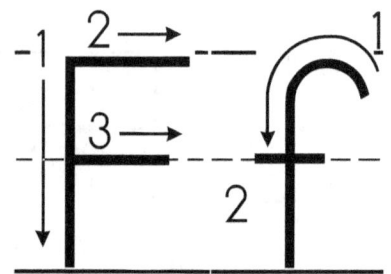

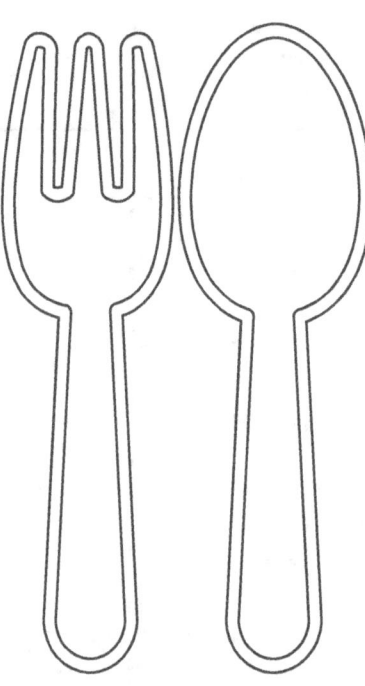

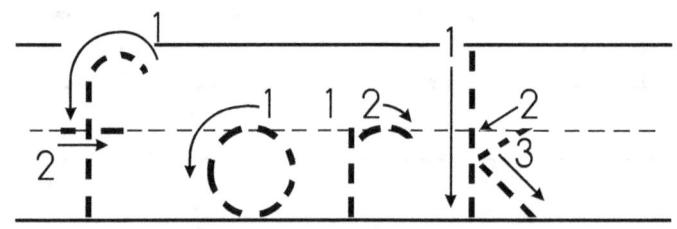

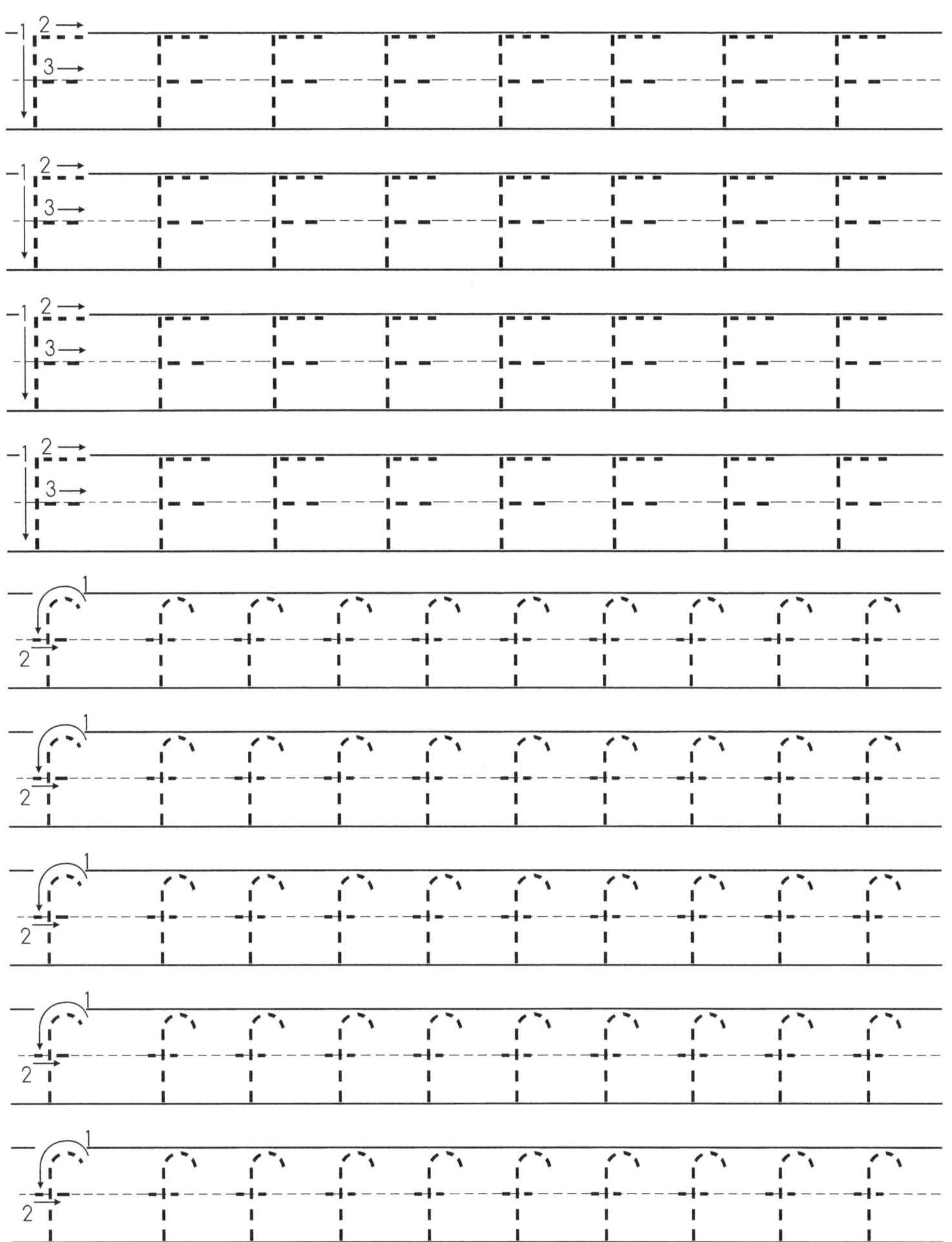

G Is For Gift

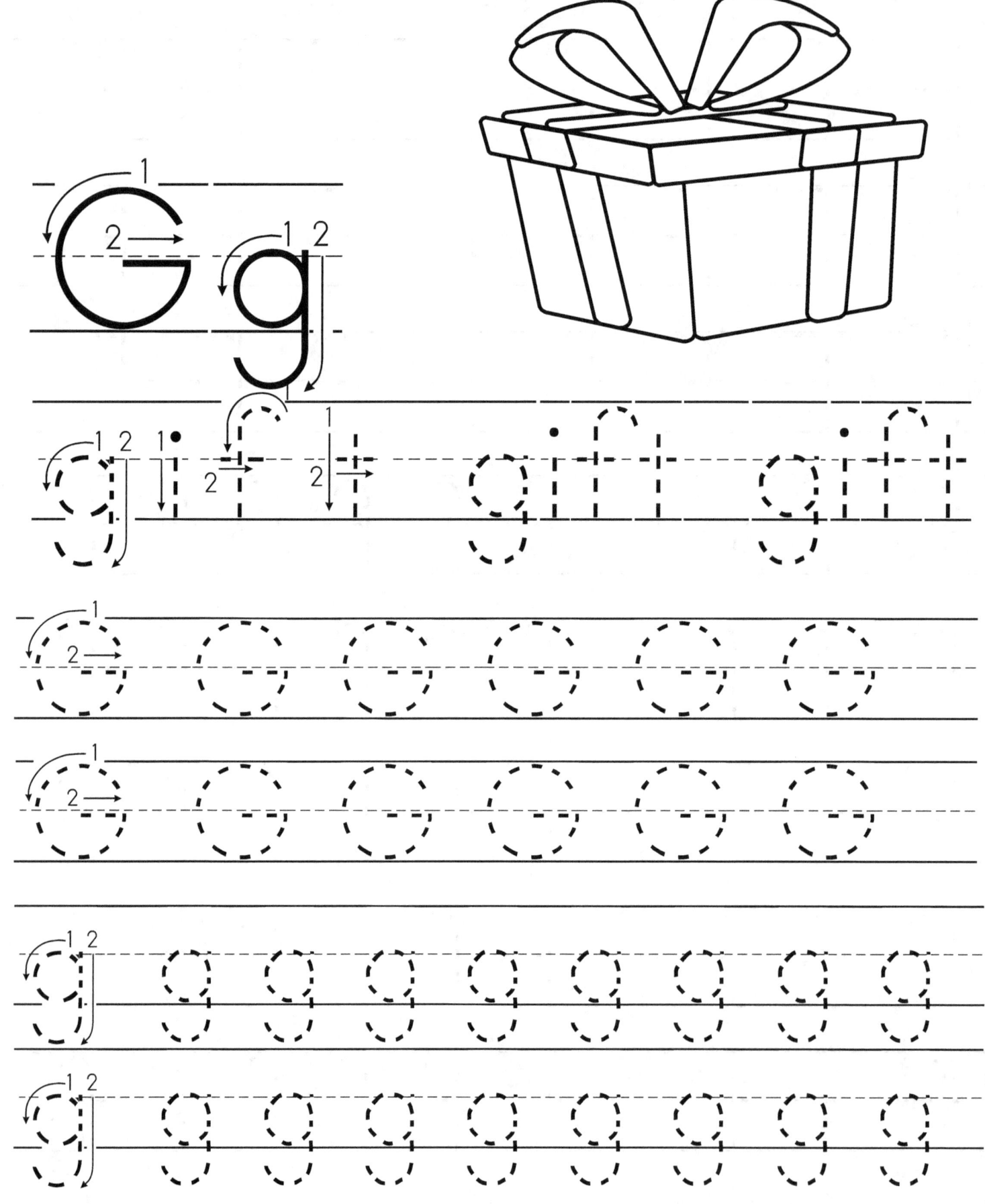

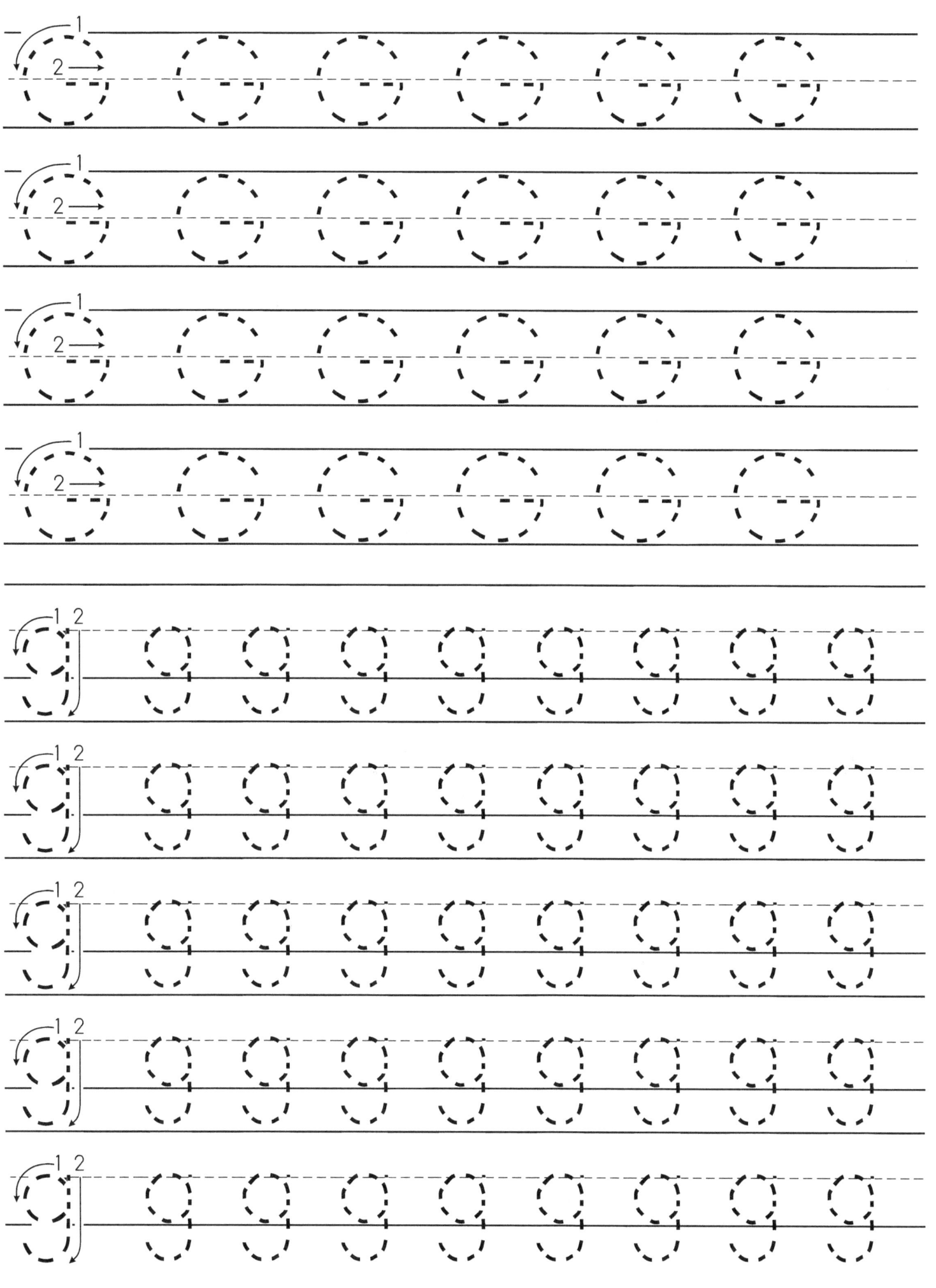

H Is For Hat

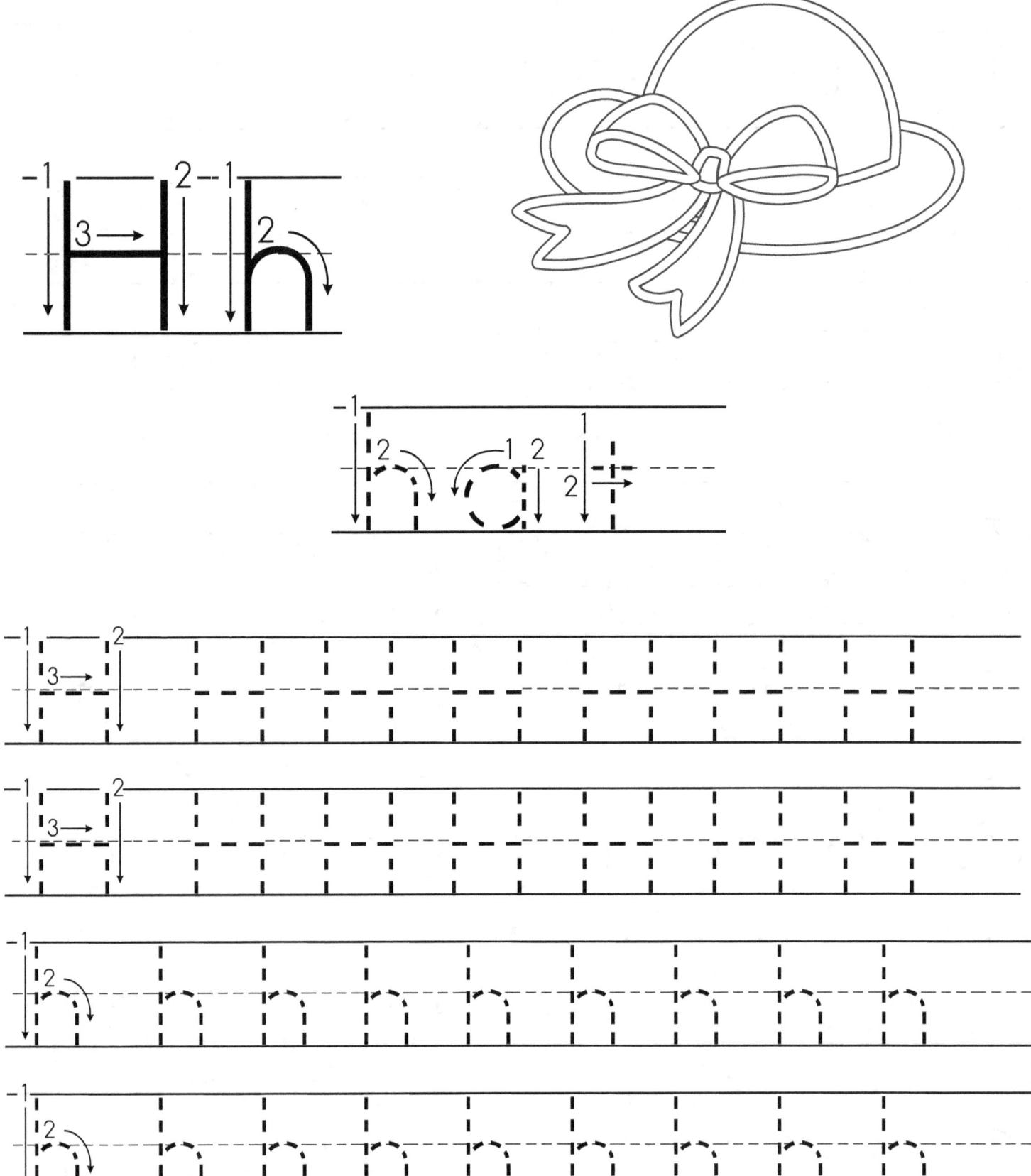

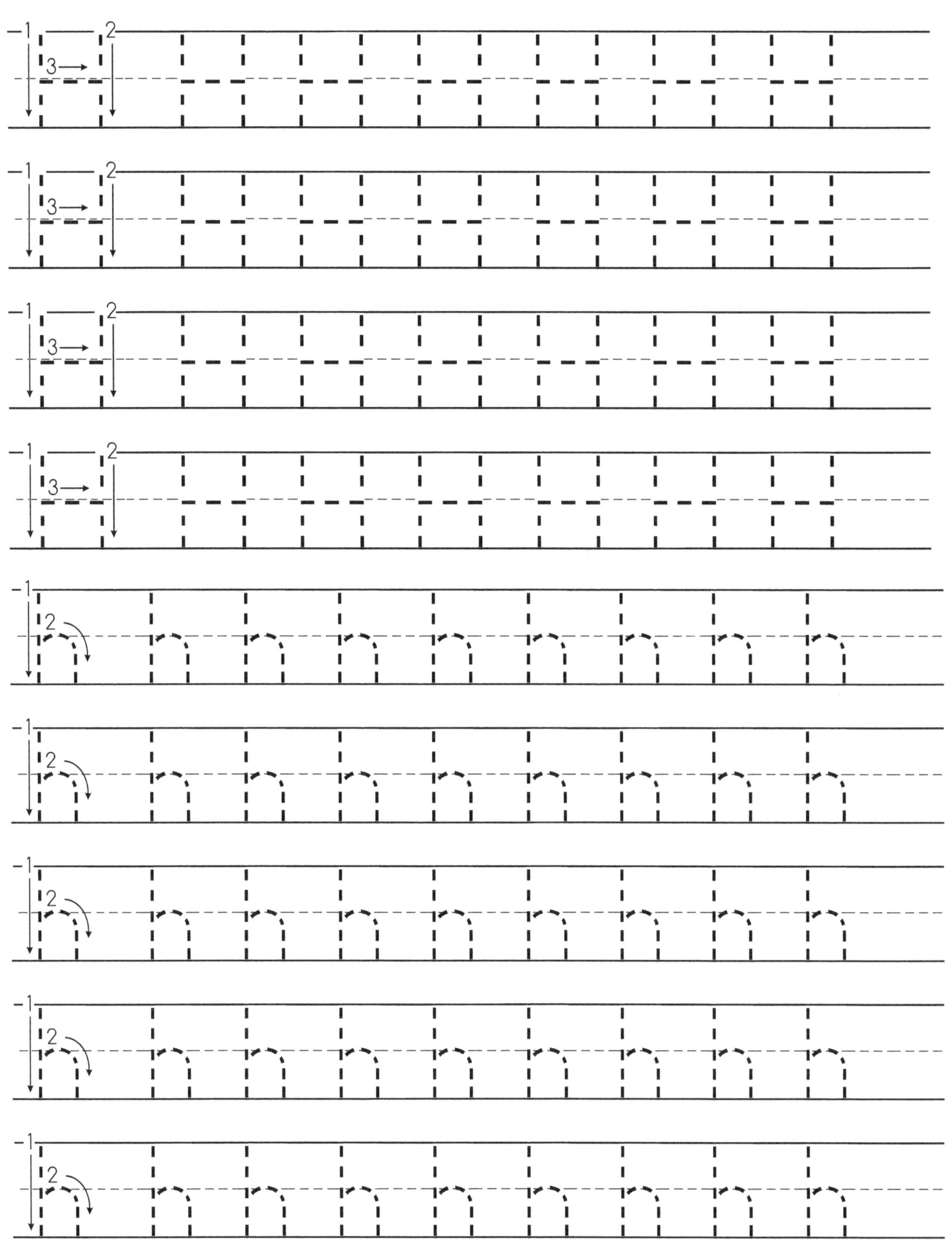

I Is For Ice

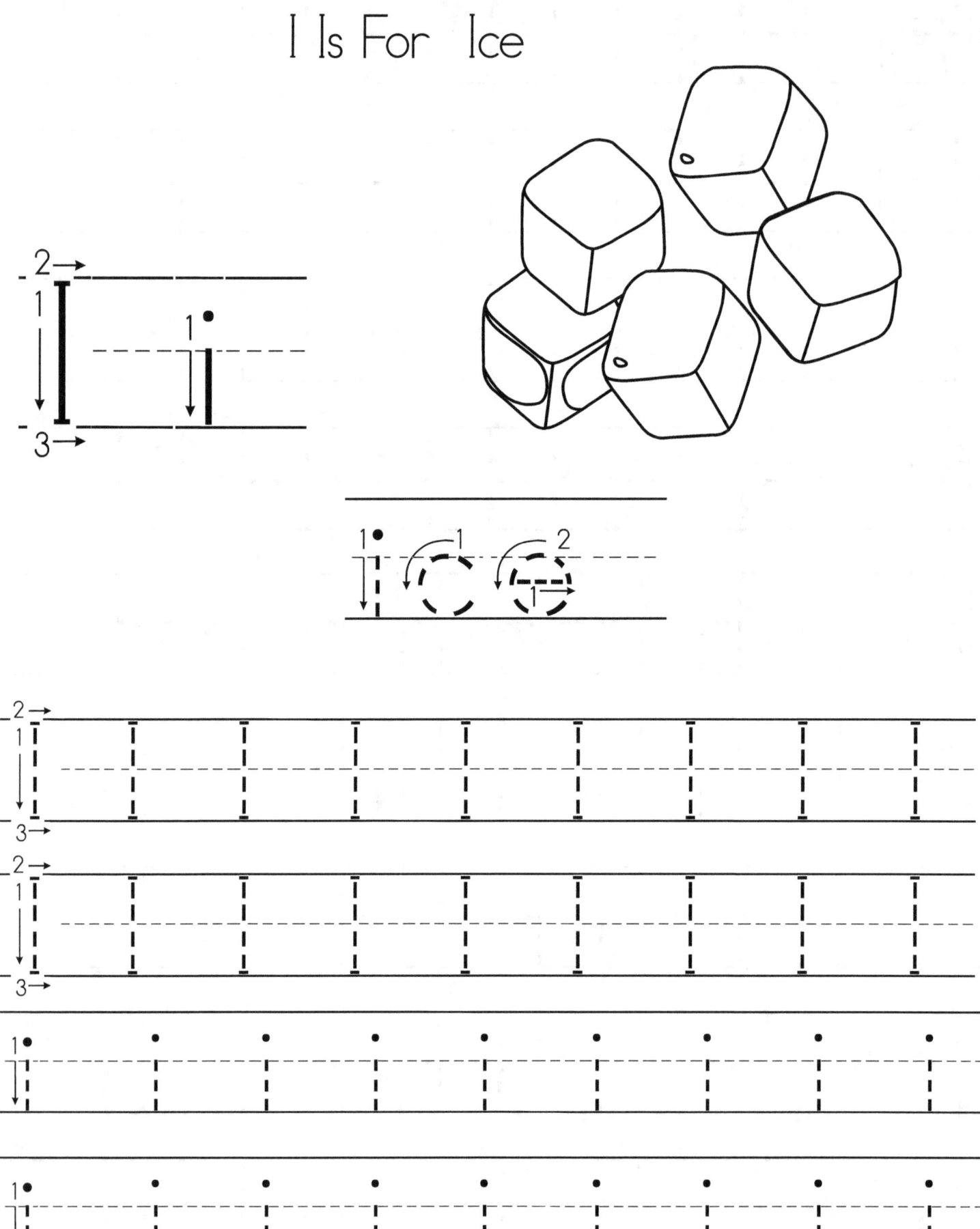

2
1
3

2
1
3

2
1
3

2
1
3

1

1

1

1

1

J Is For Jar

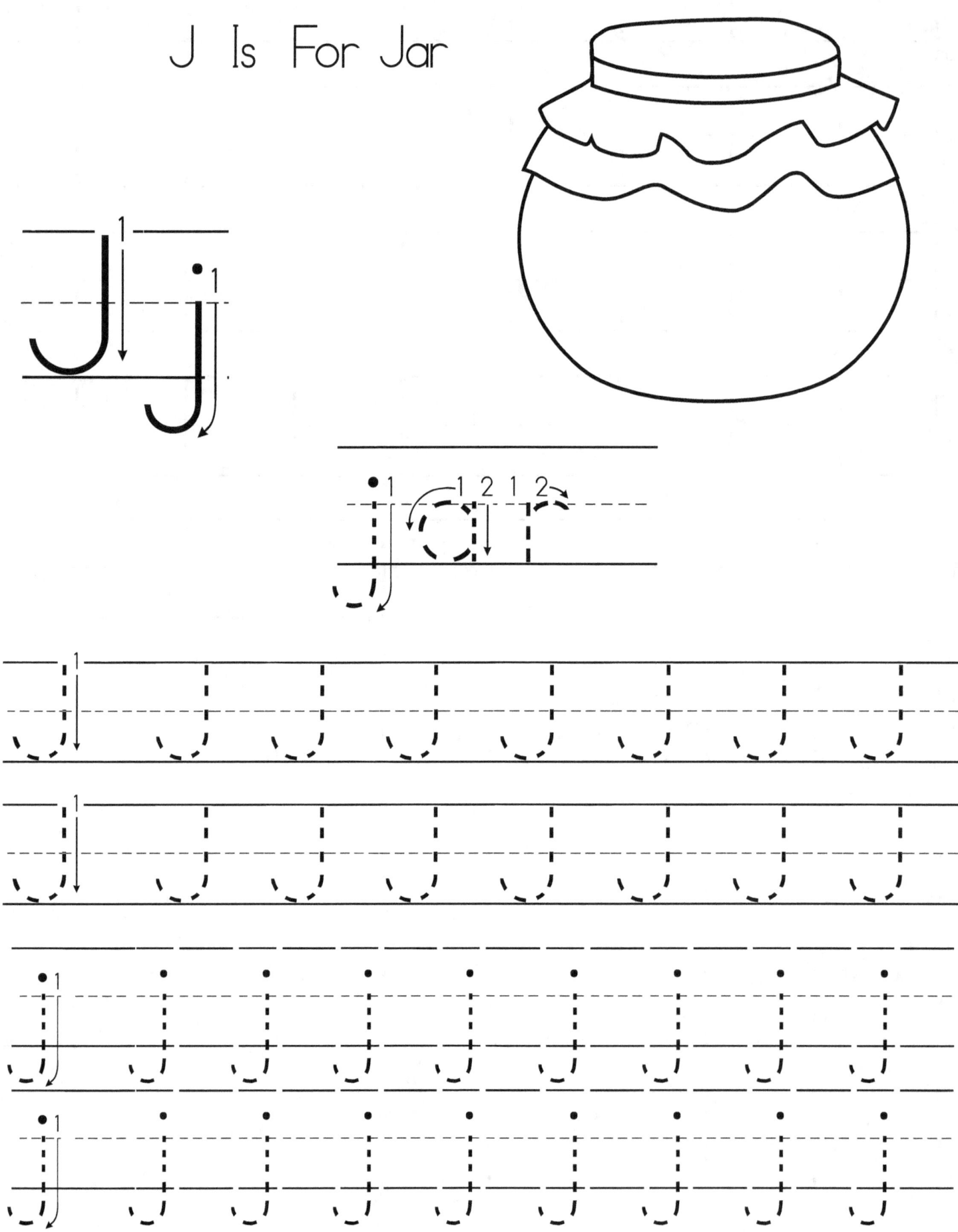

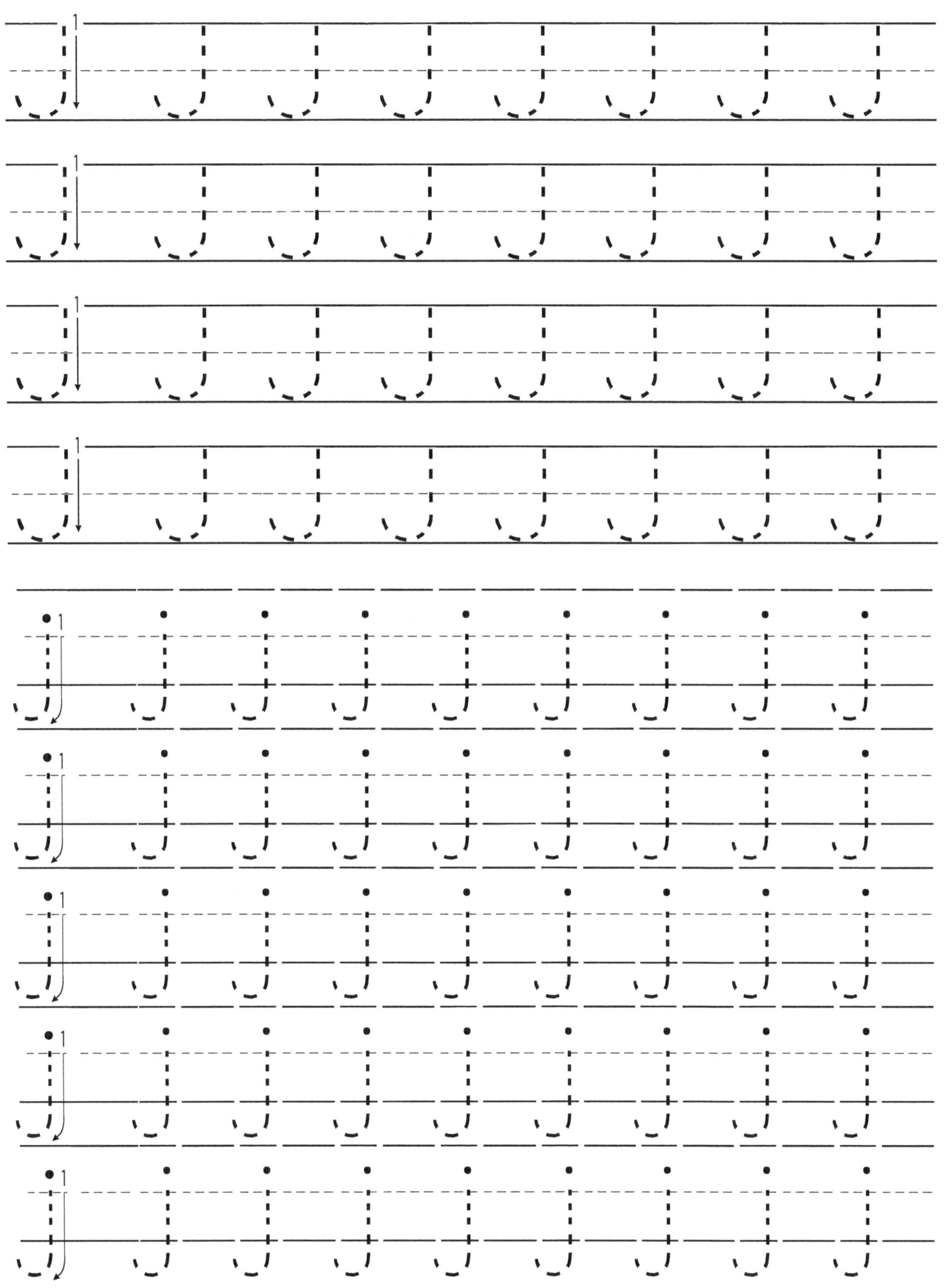

K Is For Kite

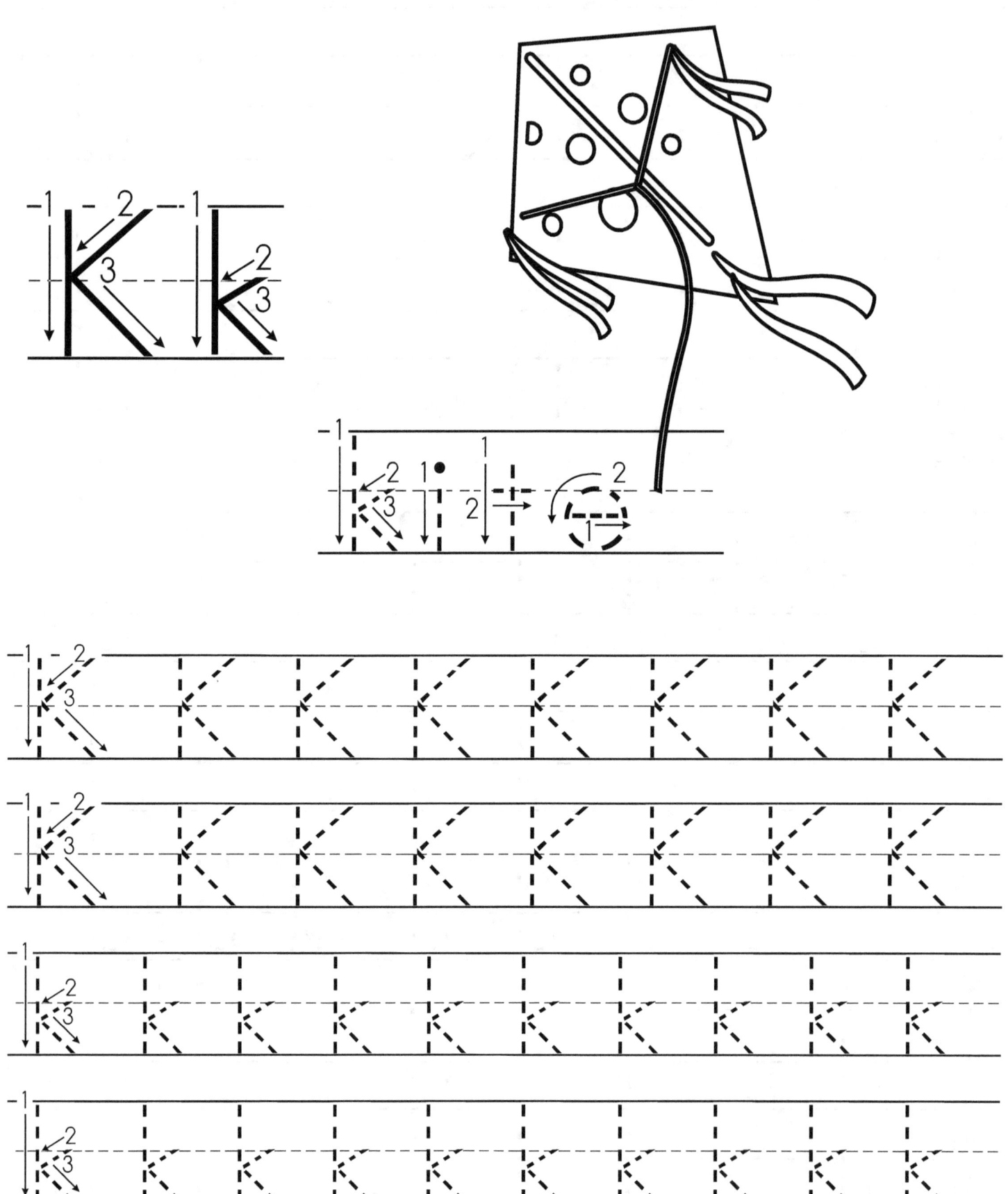

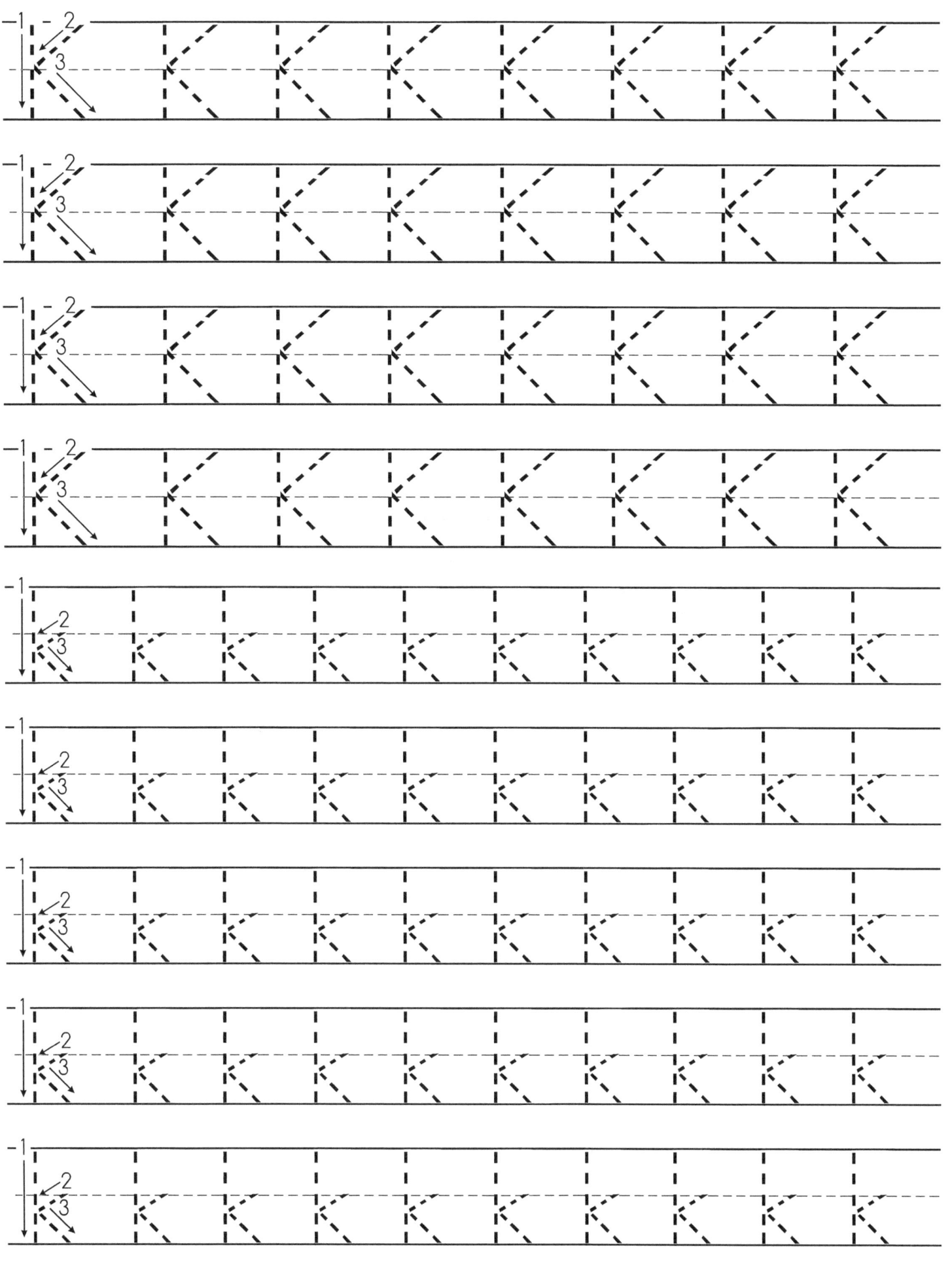

L Is For Lamp

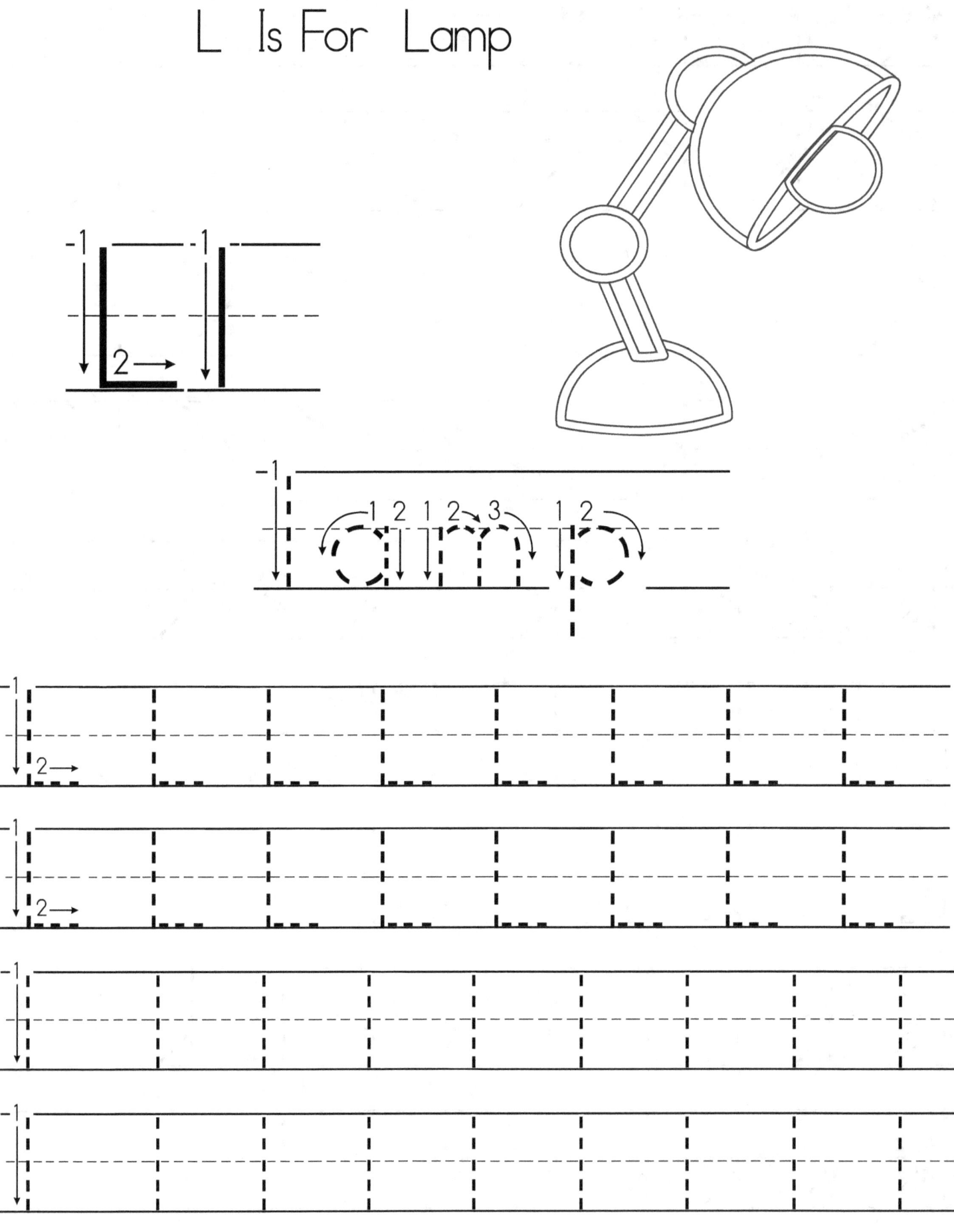

1
2

1
2

1
2

1
2

1

1

1

1

1

M Is For Mushroom

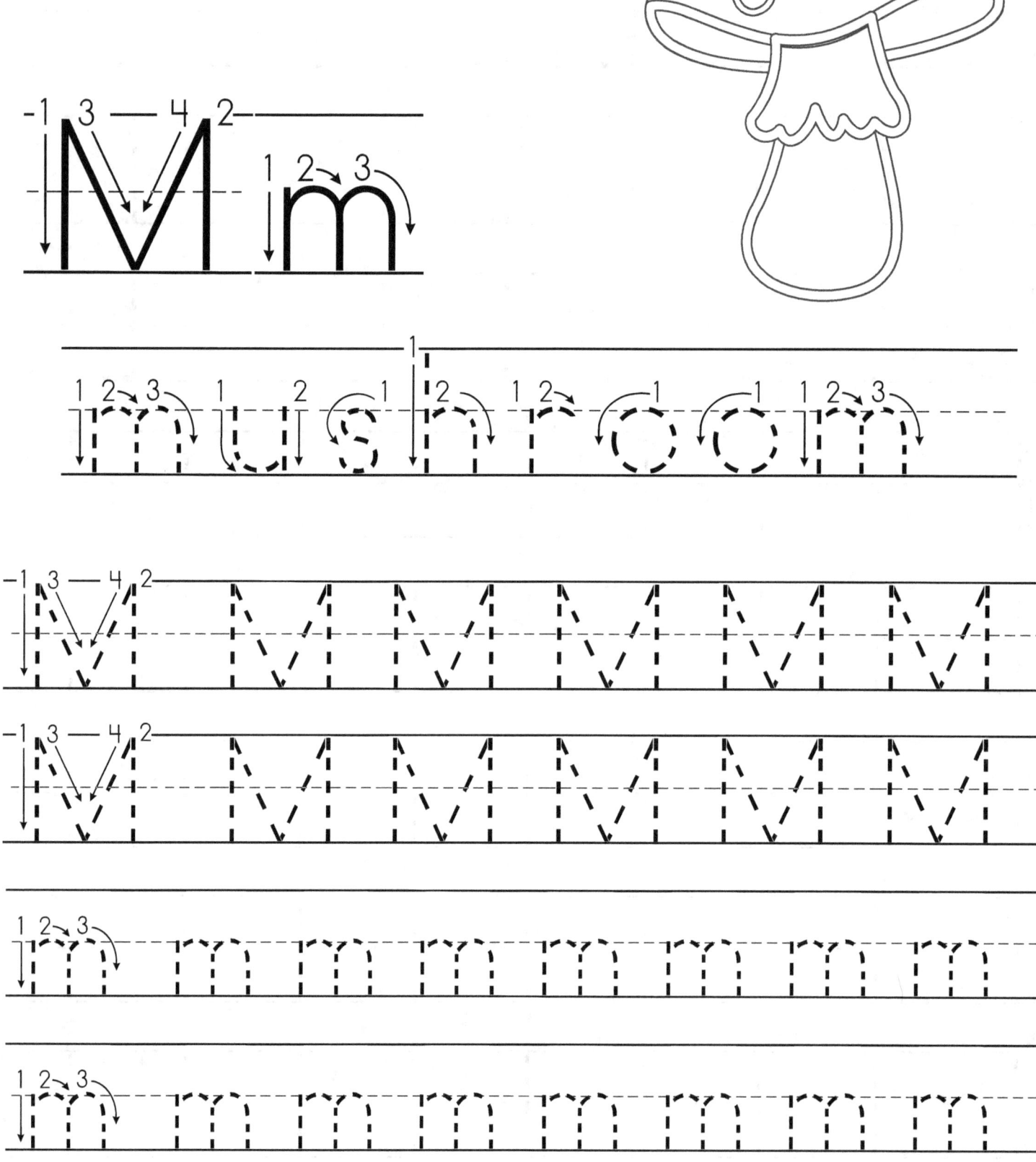

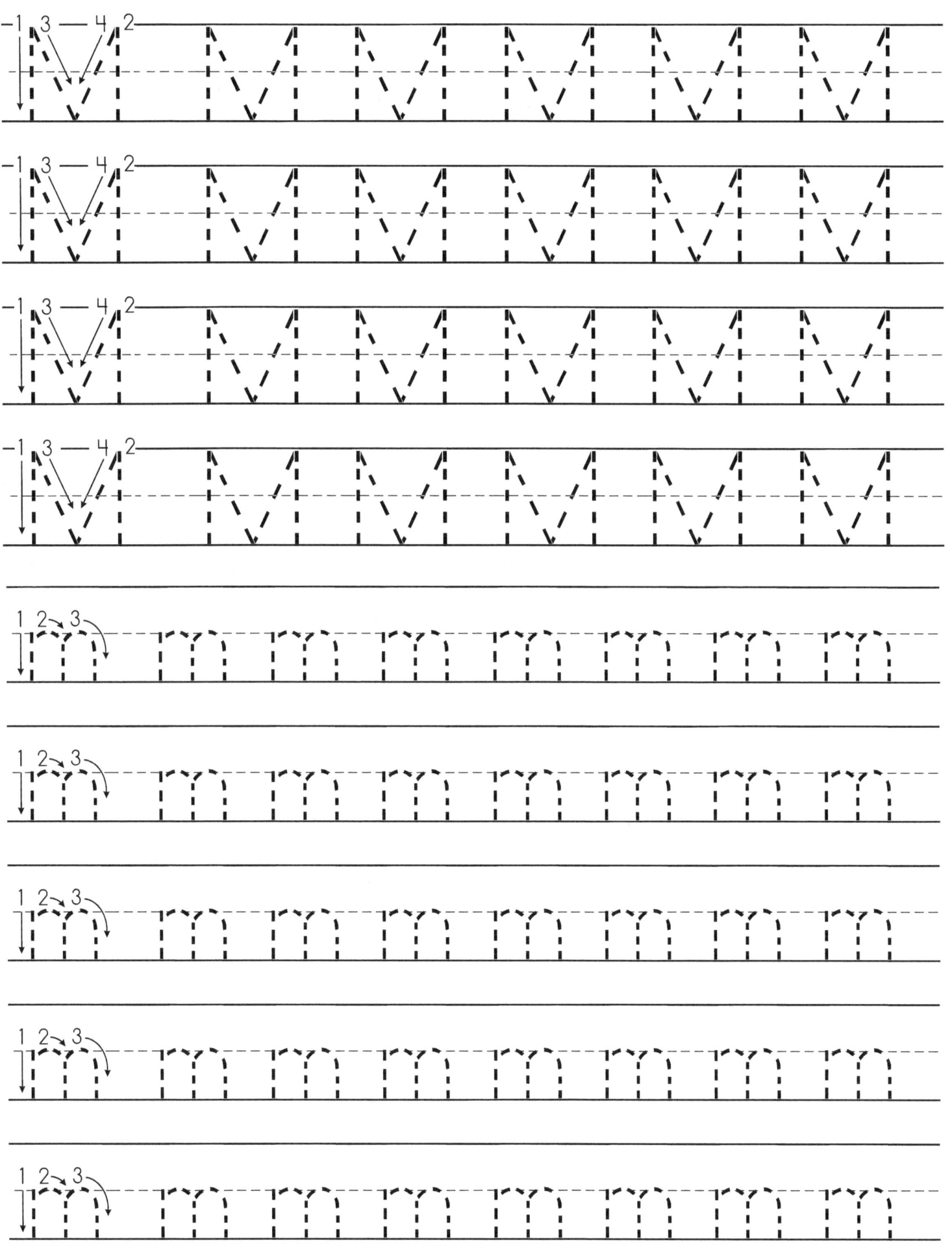

N Is For Nurse

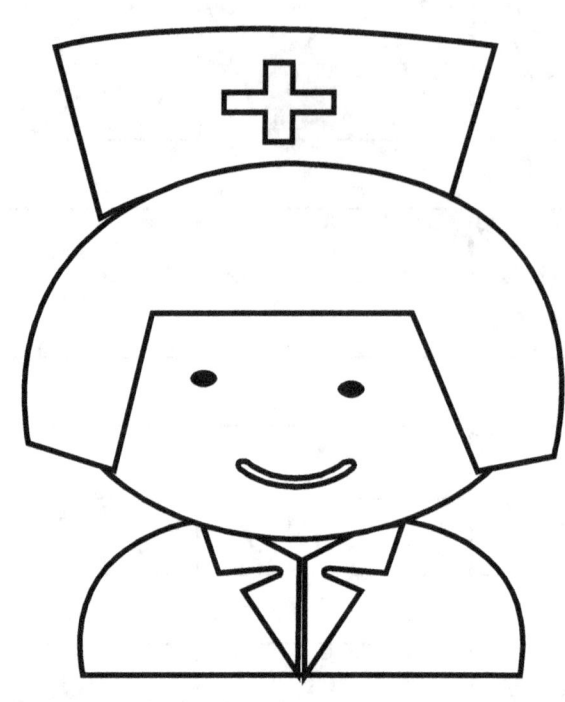

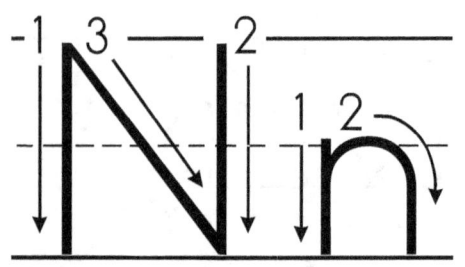

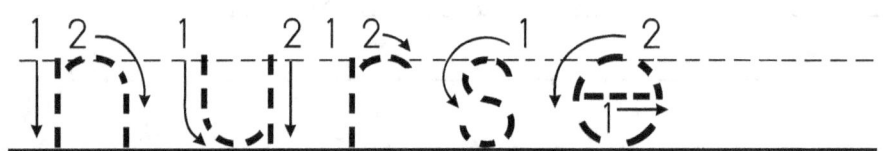

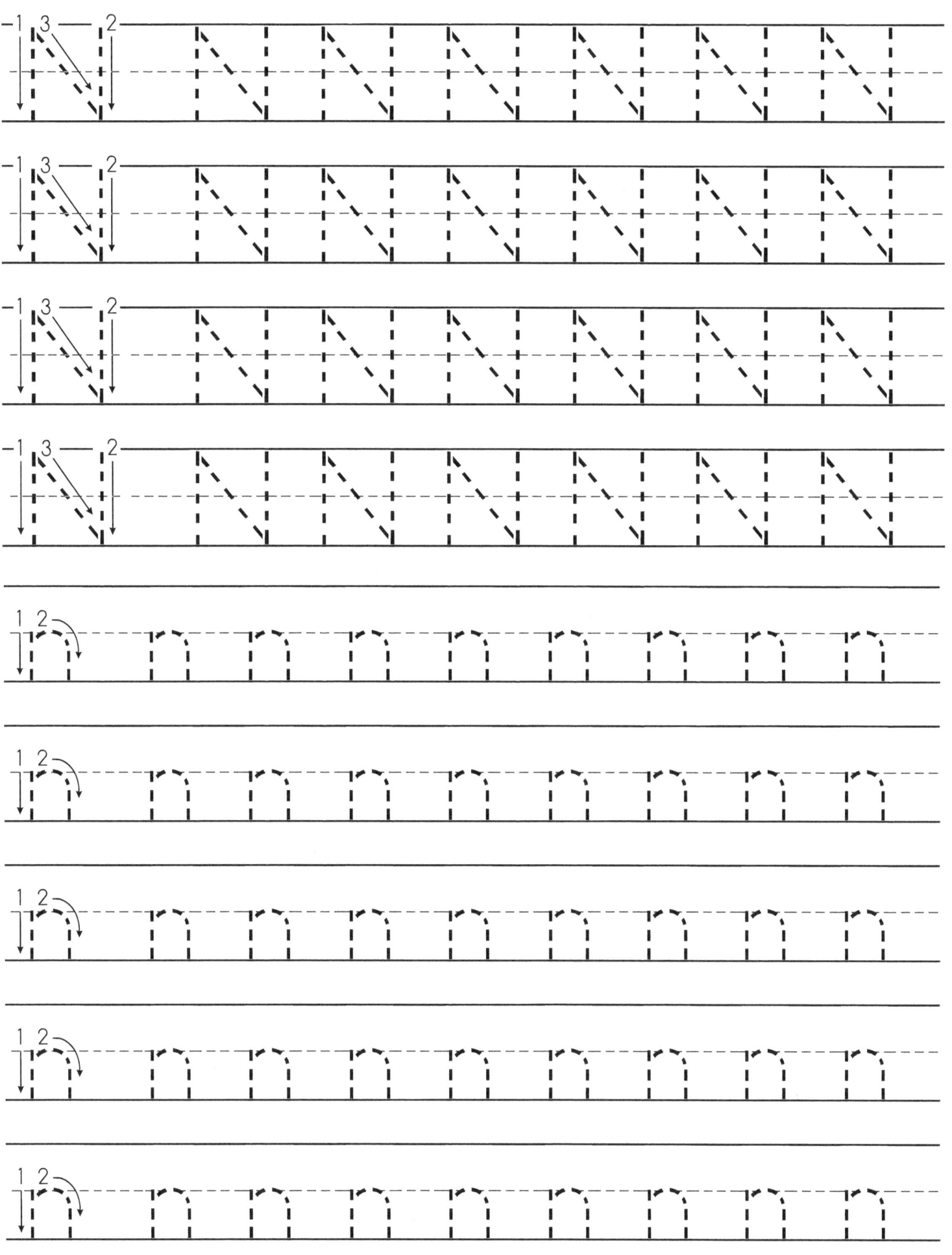

O Is For Orange

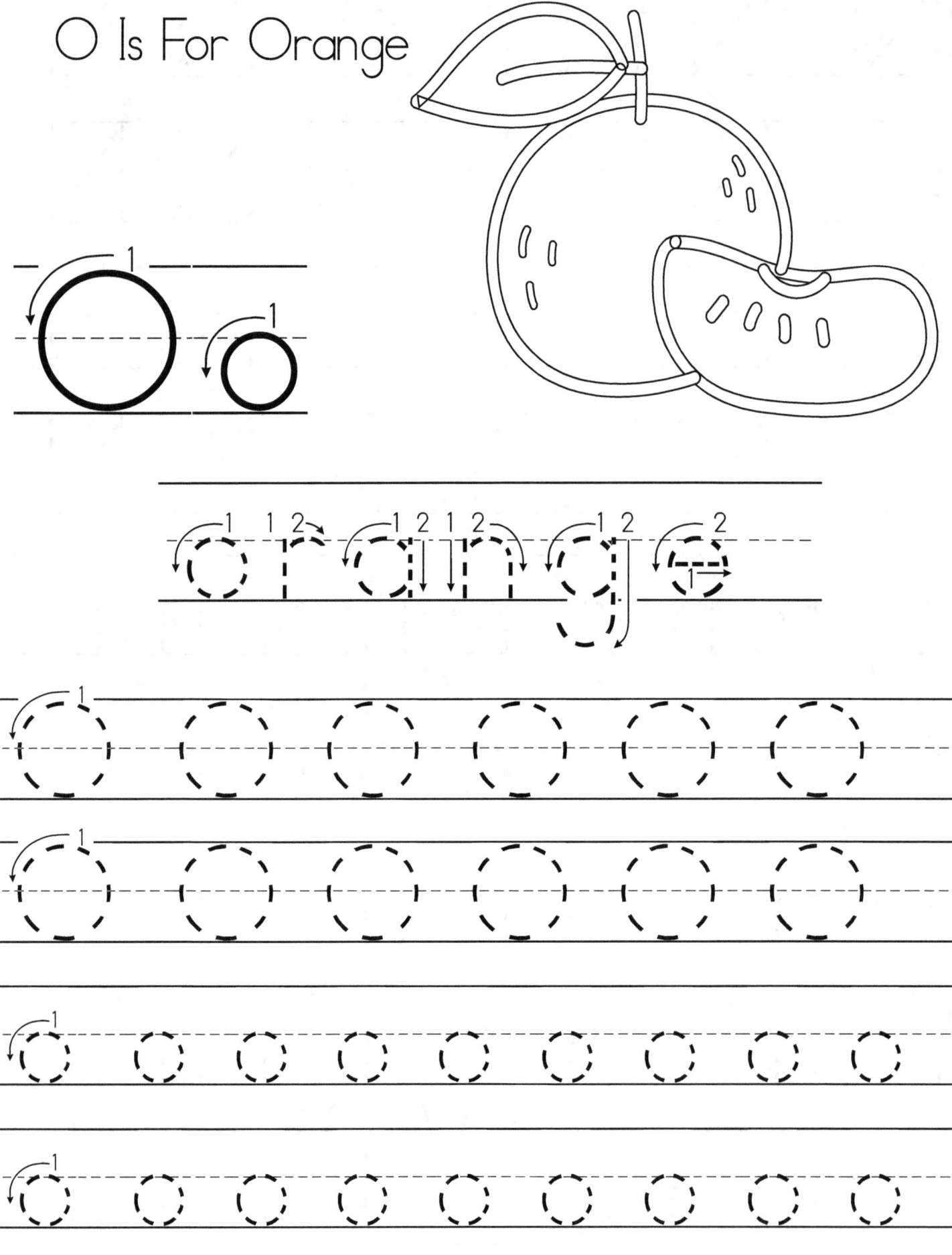

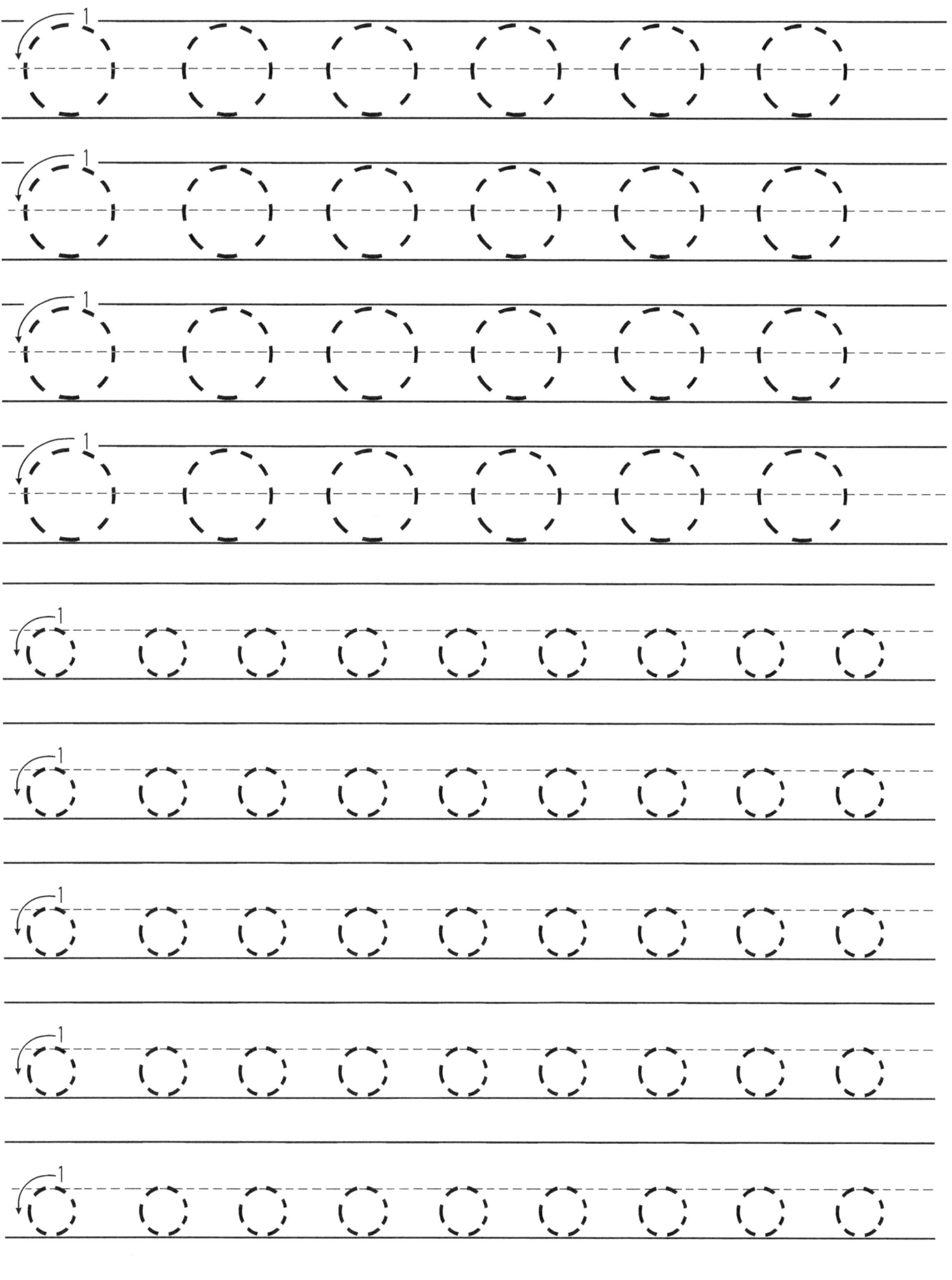

P Is For Pencil

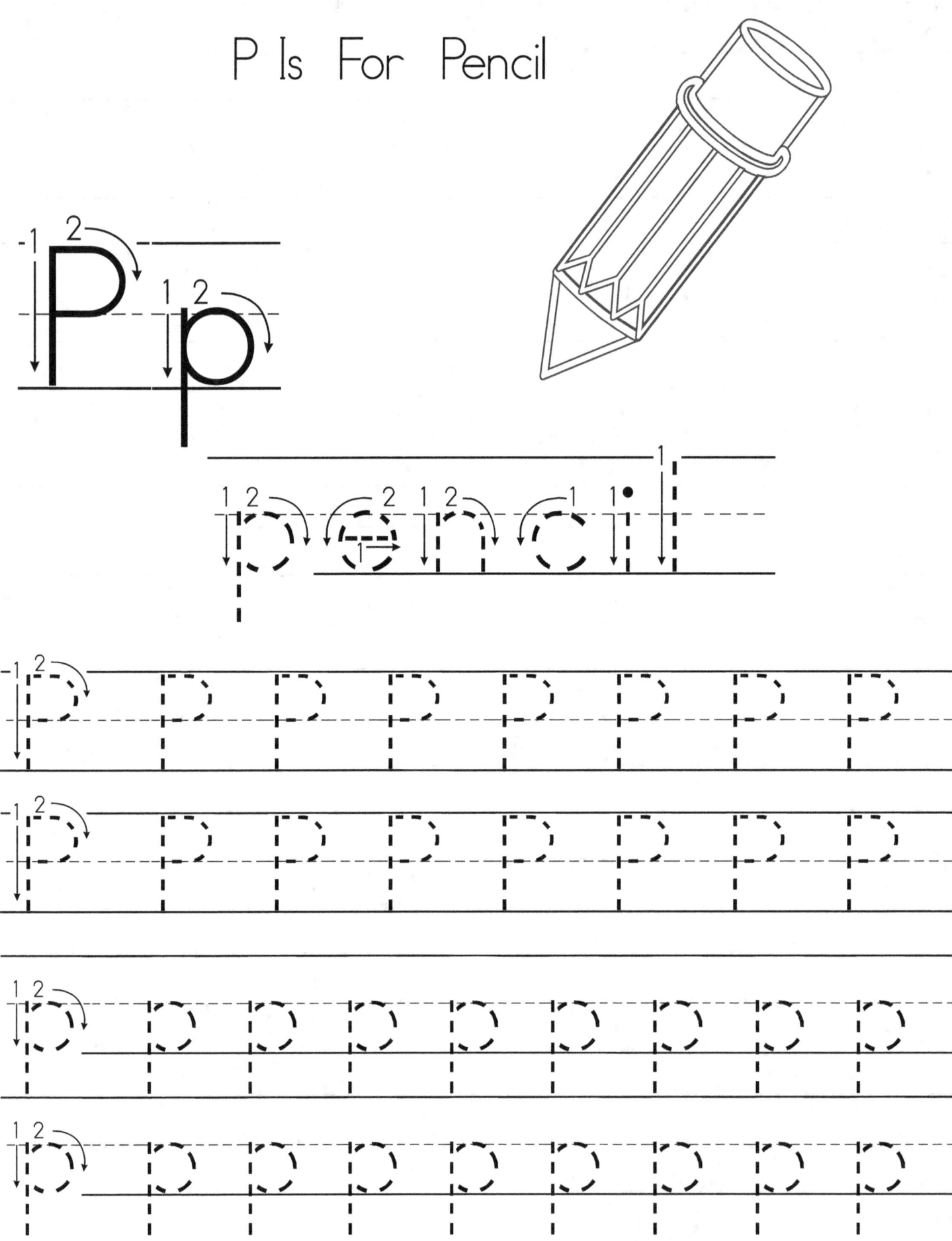

P

-1 2 P P P P P P P P P

-1 2 P P P P P P P P P

-1 2 P P P P P P P P P

-1 2 P P P P P P P P P

1 2 p p p p p p p p p

1 2 p p p p p p p p p

1 2 p p p p p p p p p

1 2 p p p p p p p p p

1 2 p p p p p p p p p

Q Is For Queen

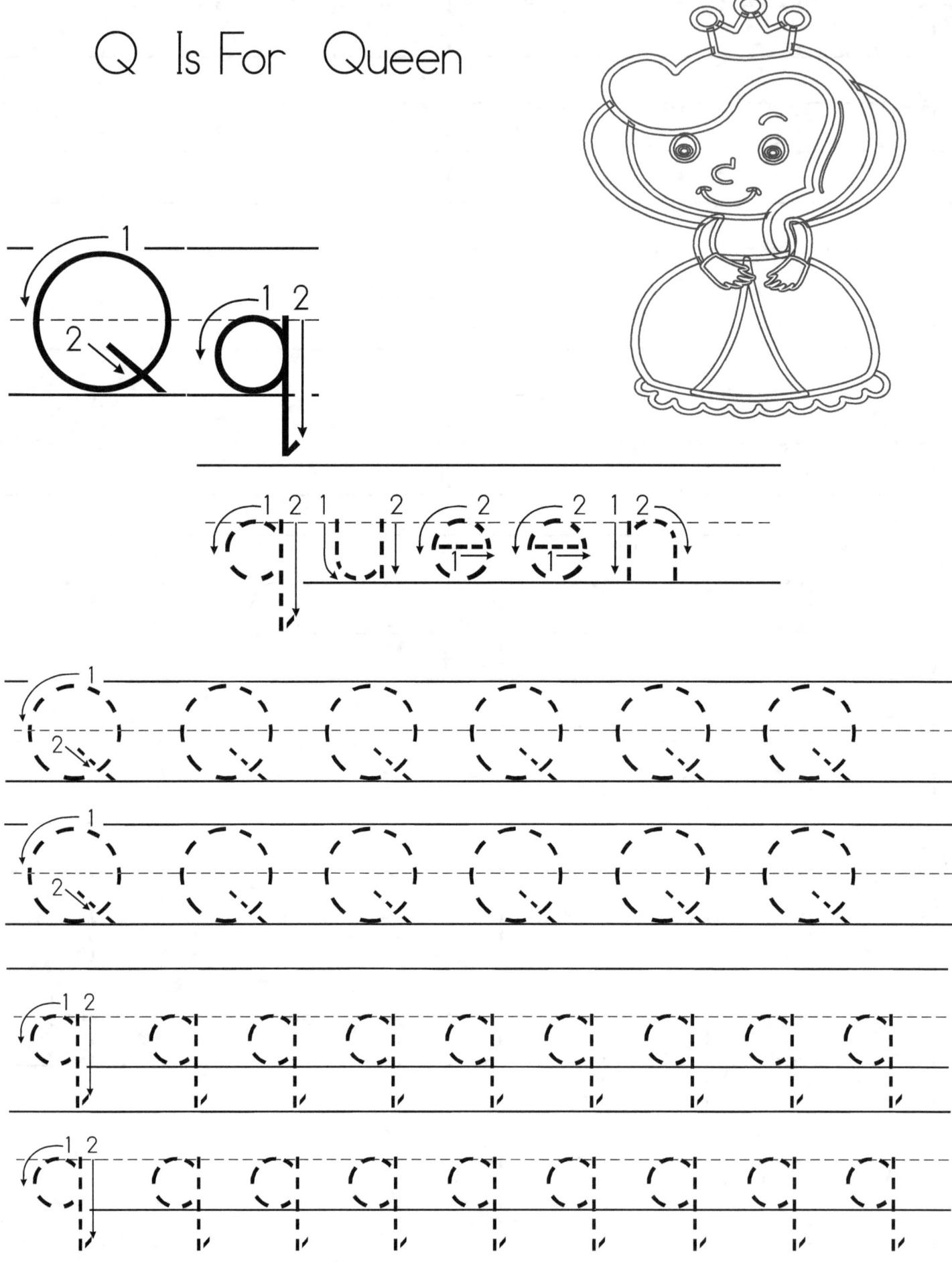

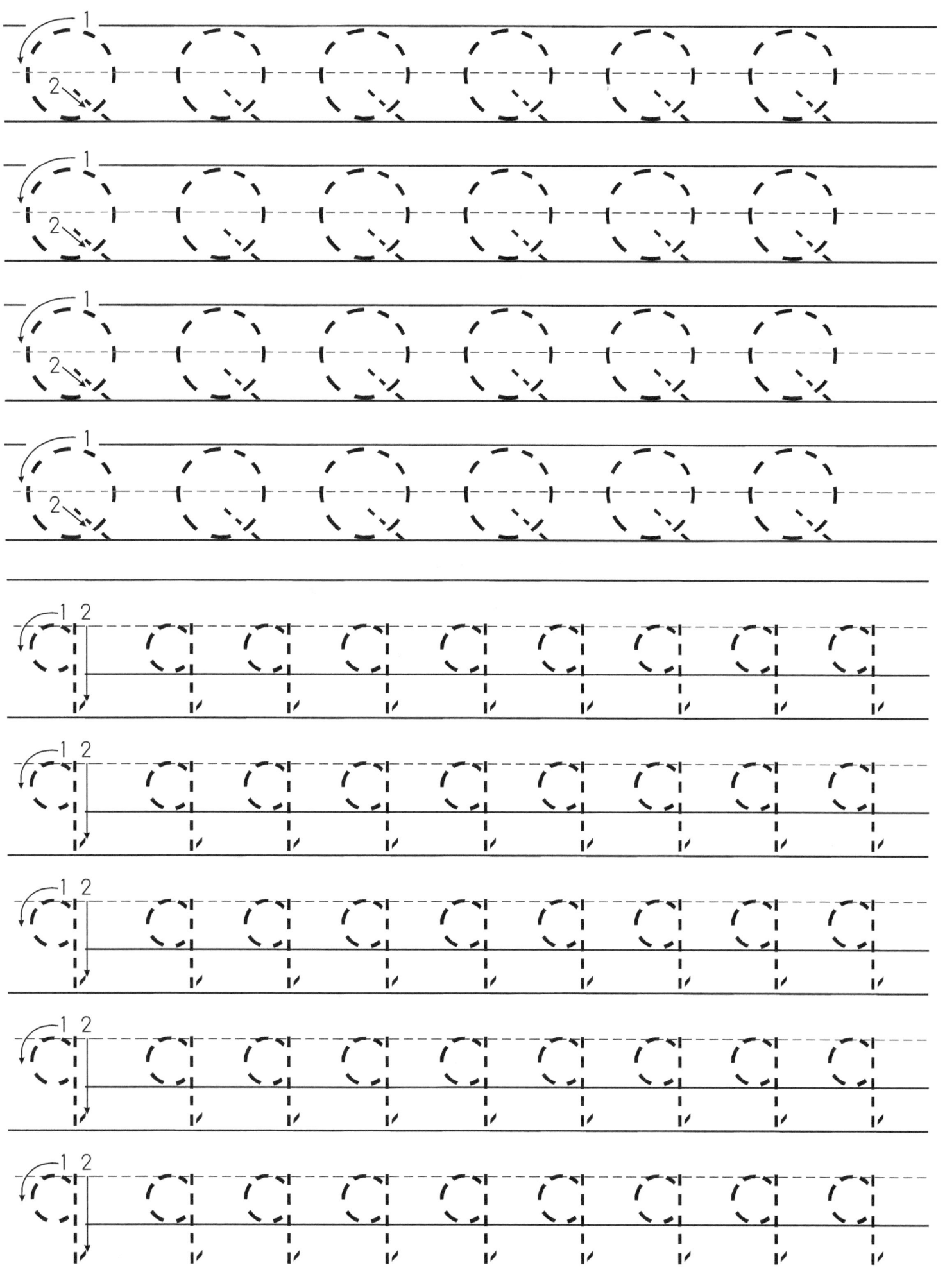

R Is For Rocket

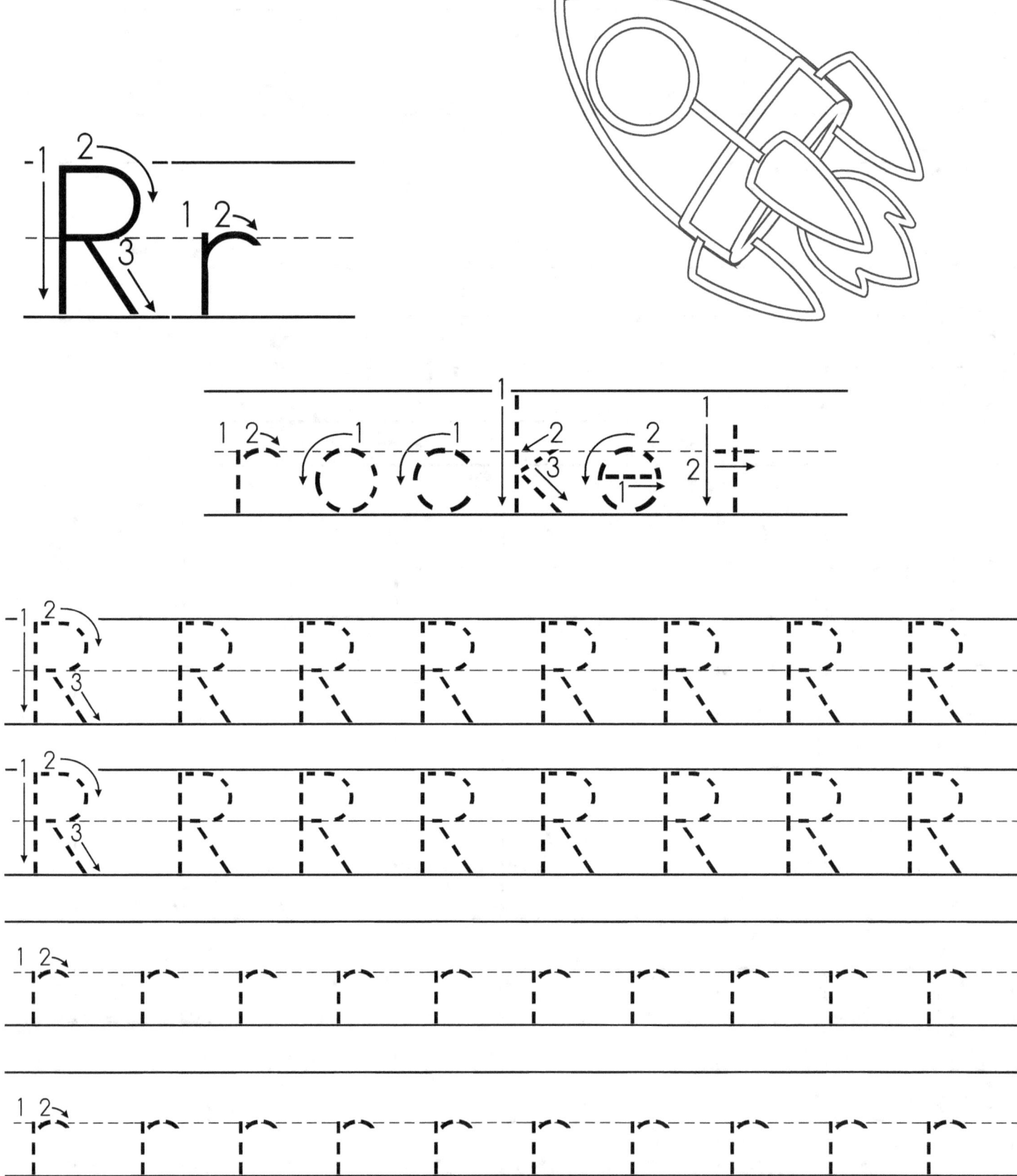

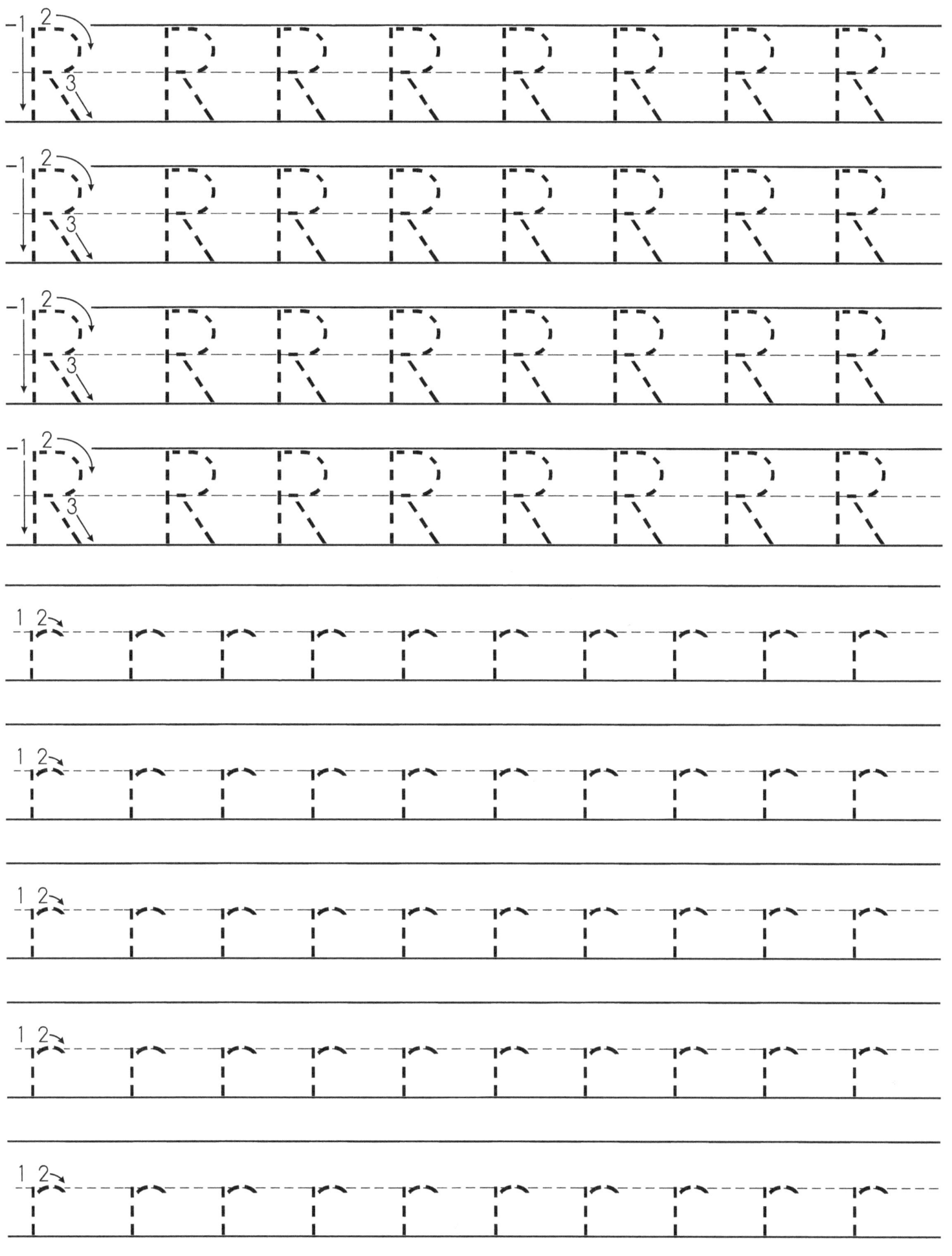

S Is For Sock

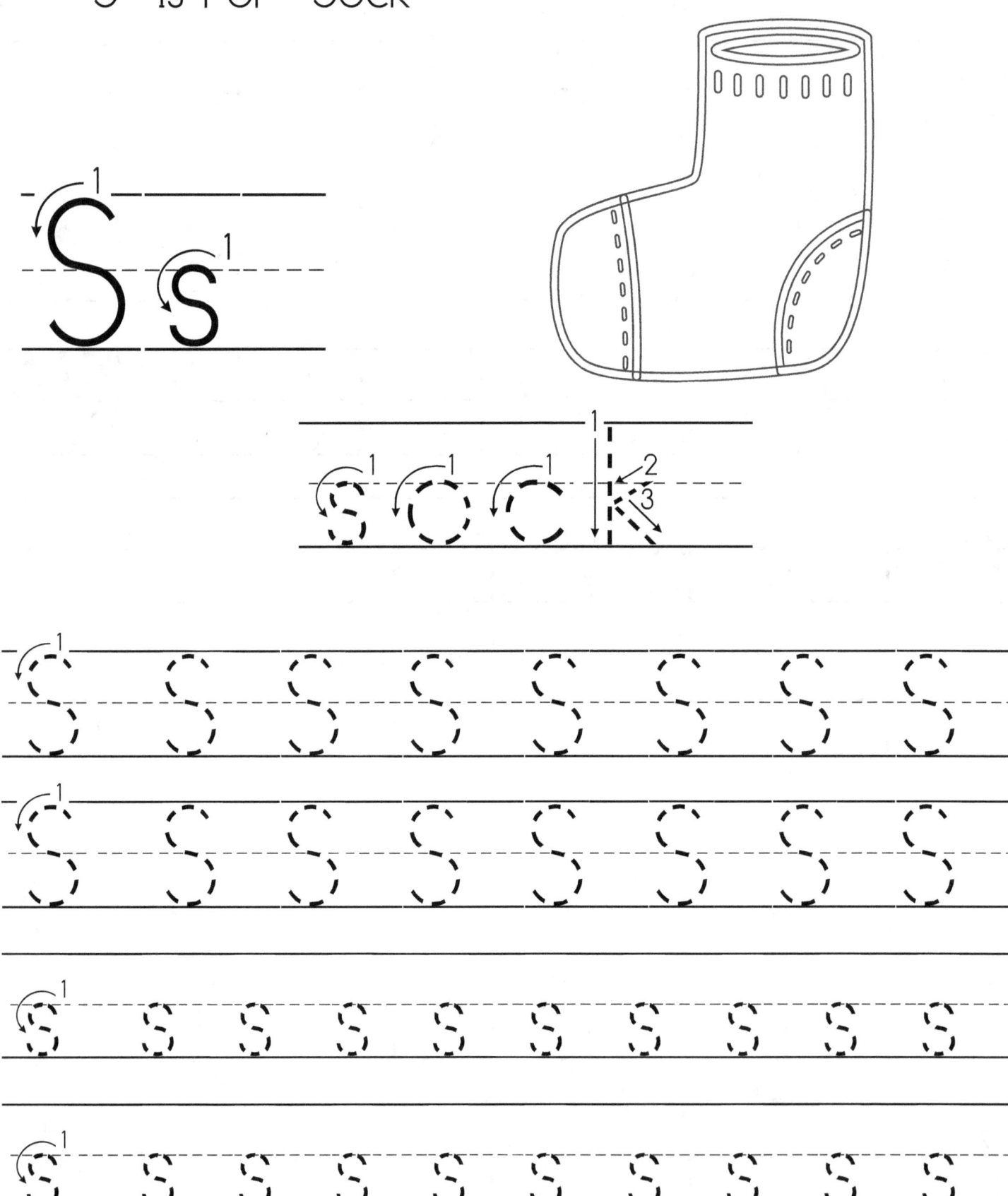

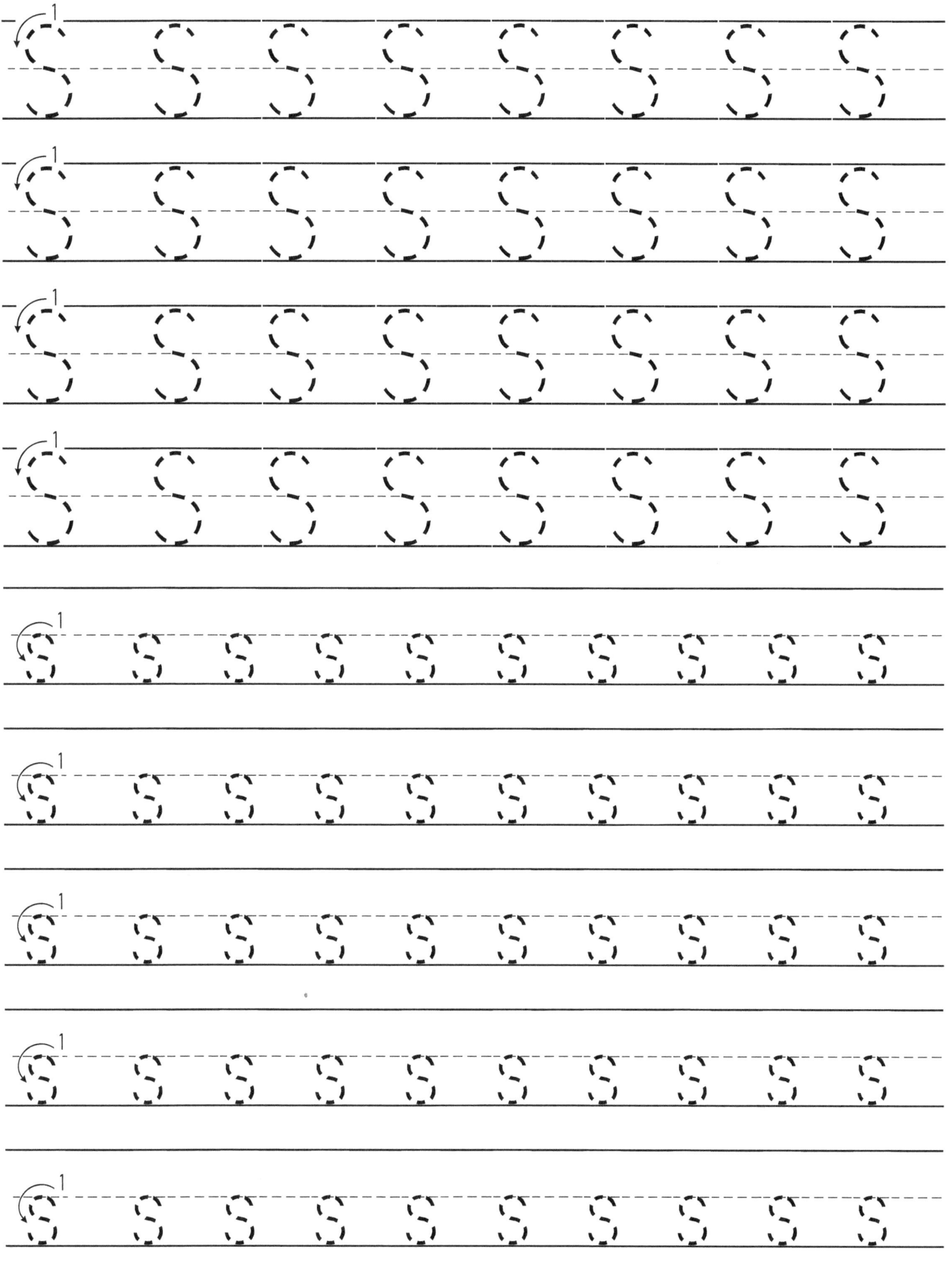

T Is for Telephone

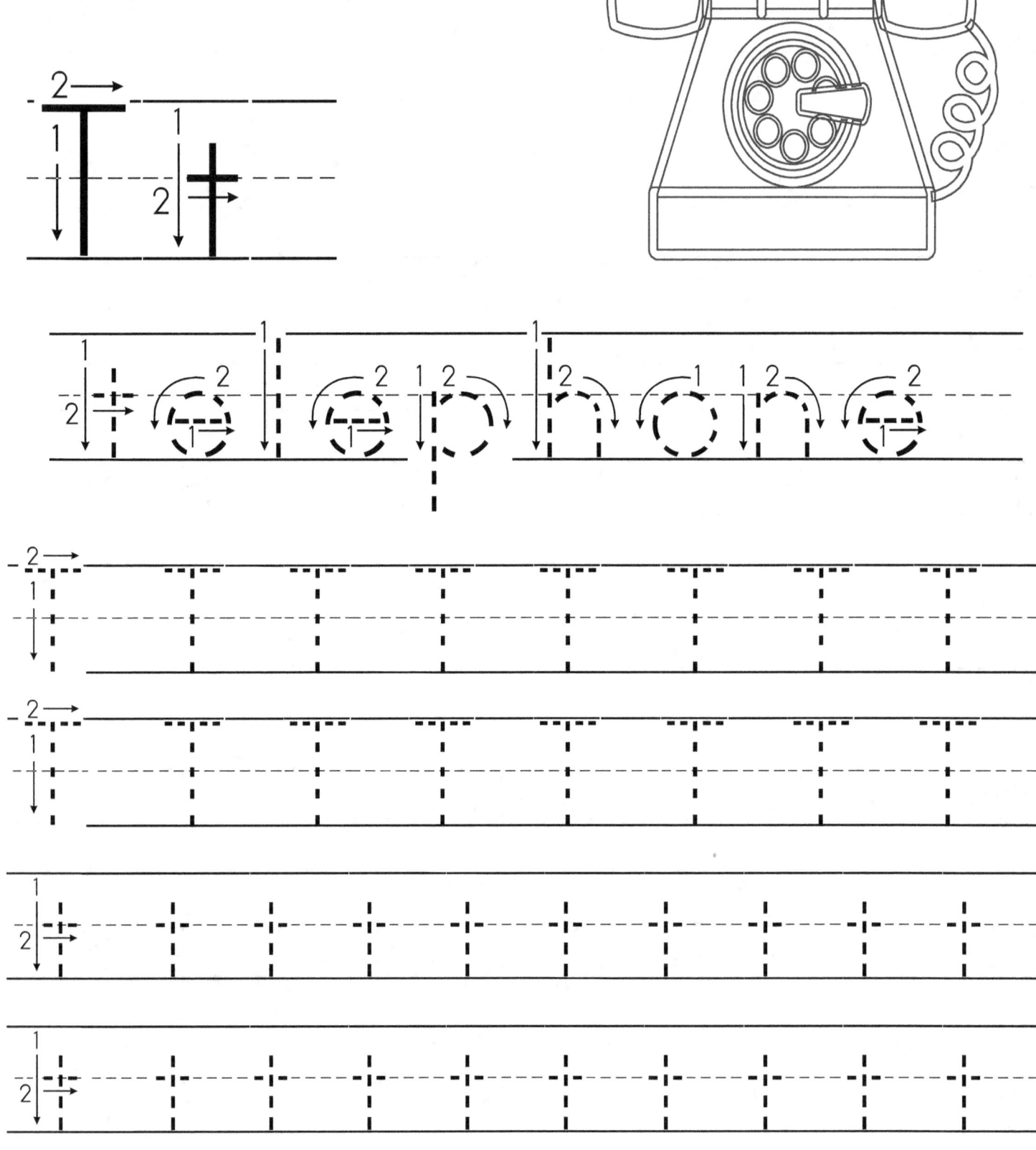

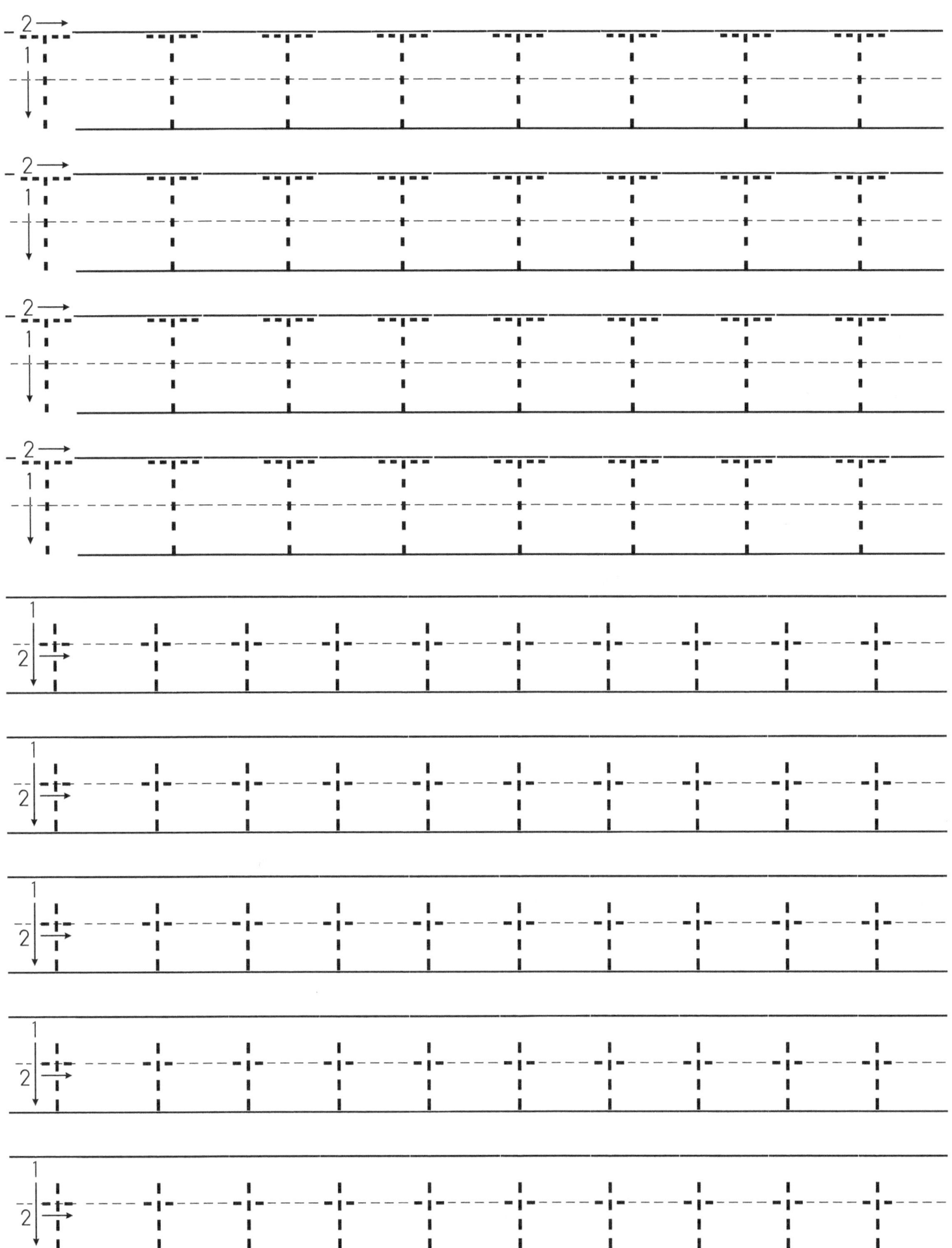

U Is For Umbrella

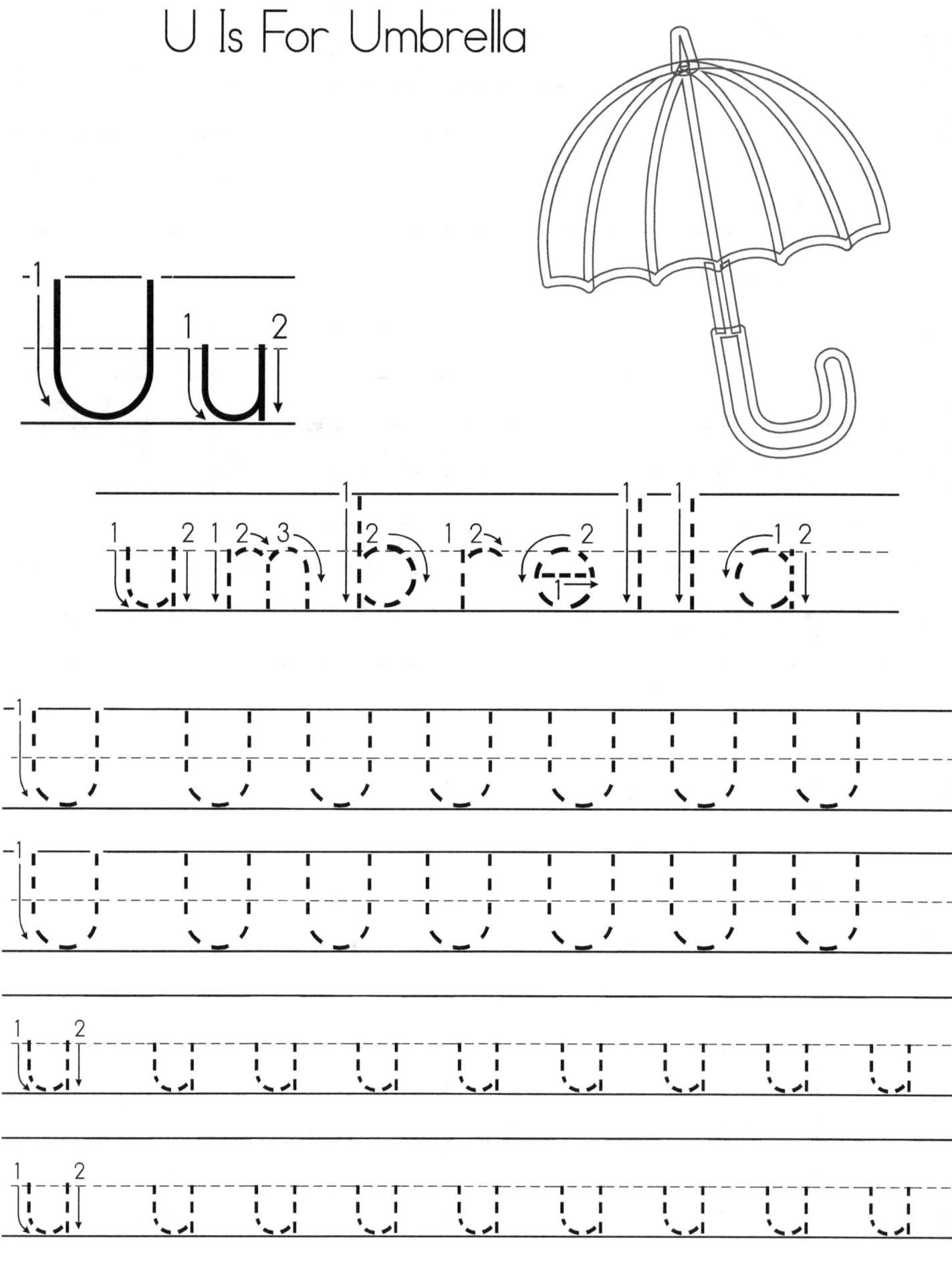

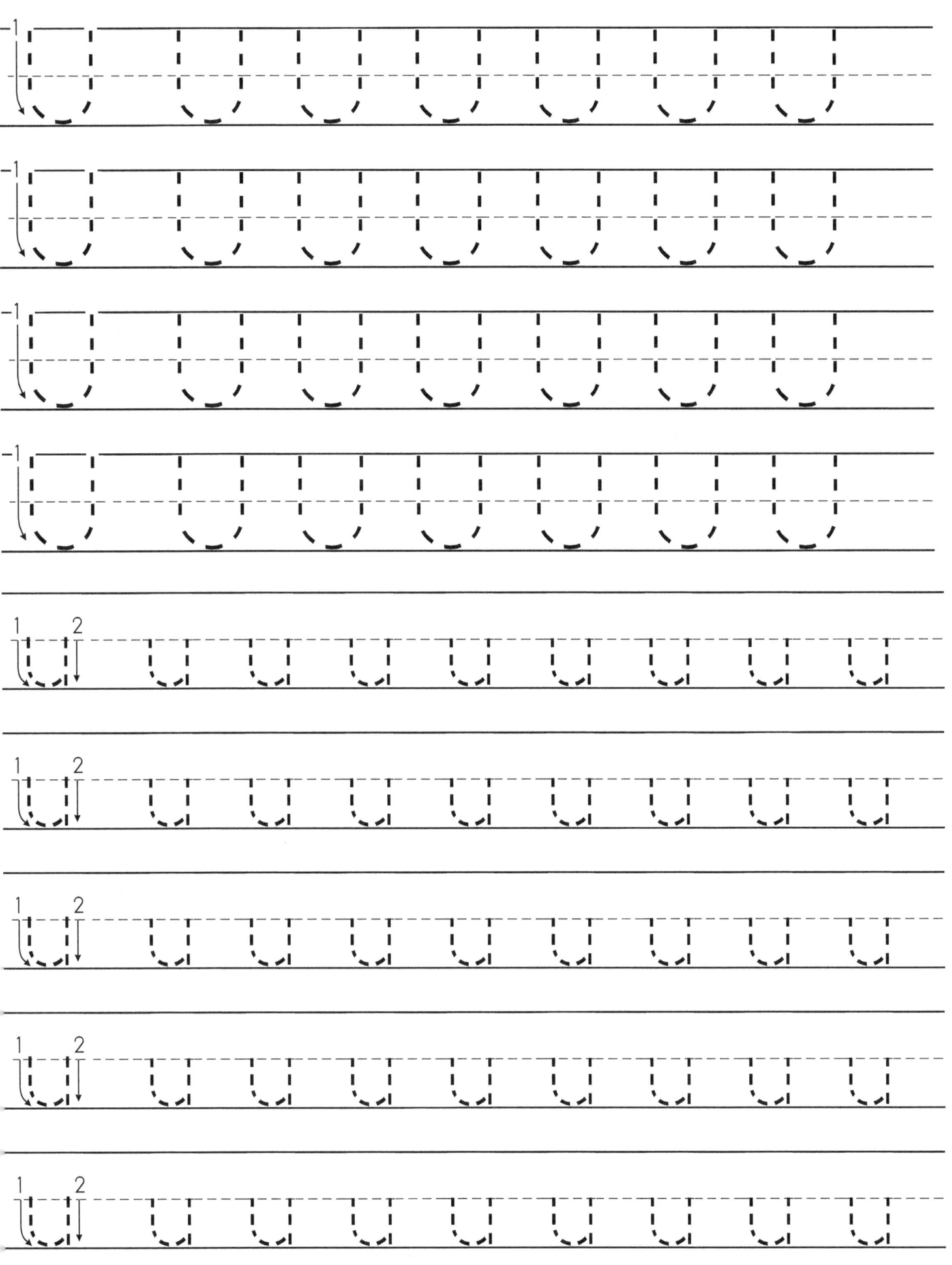

V Is For Video

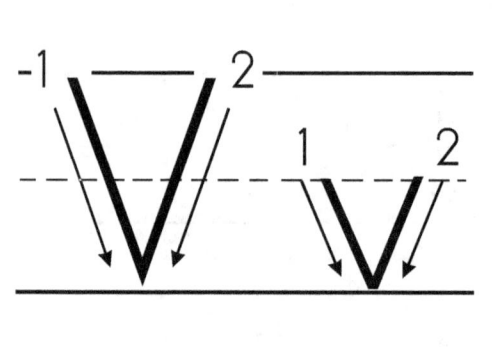

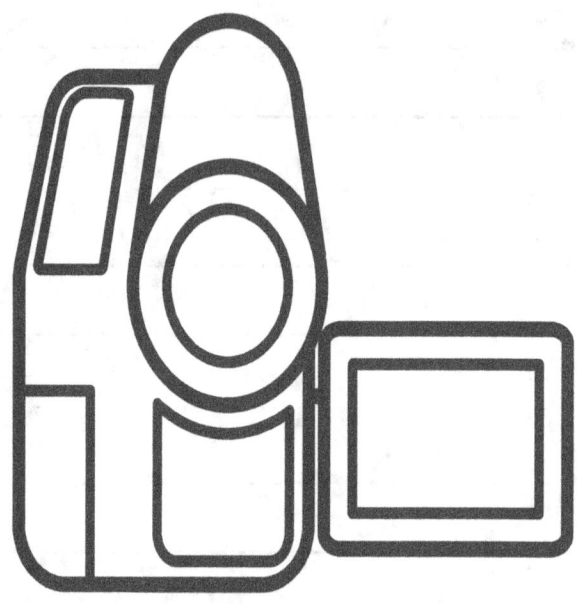

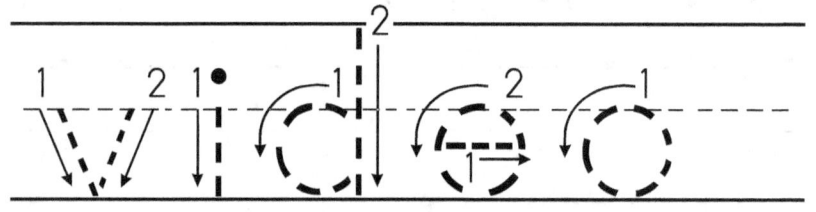

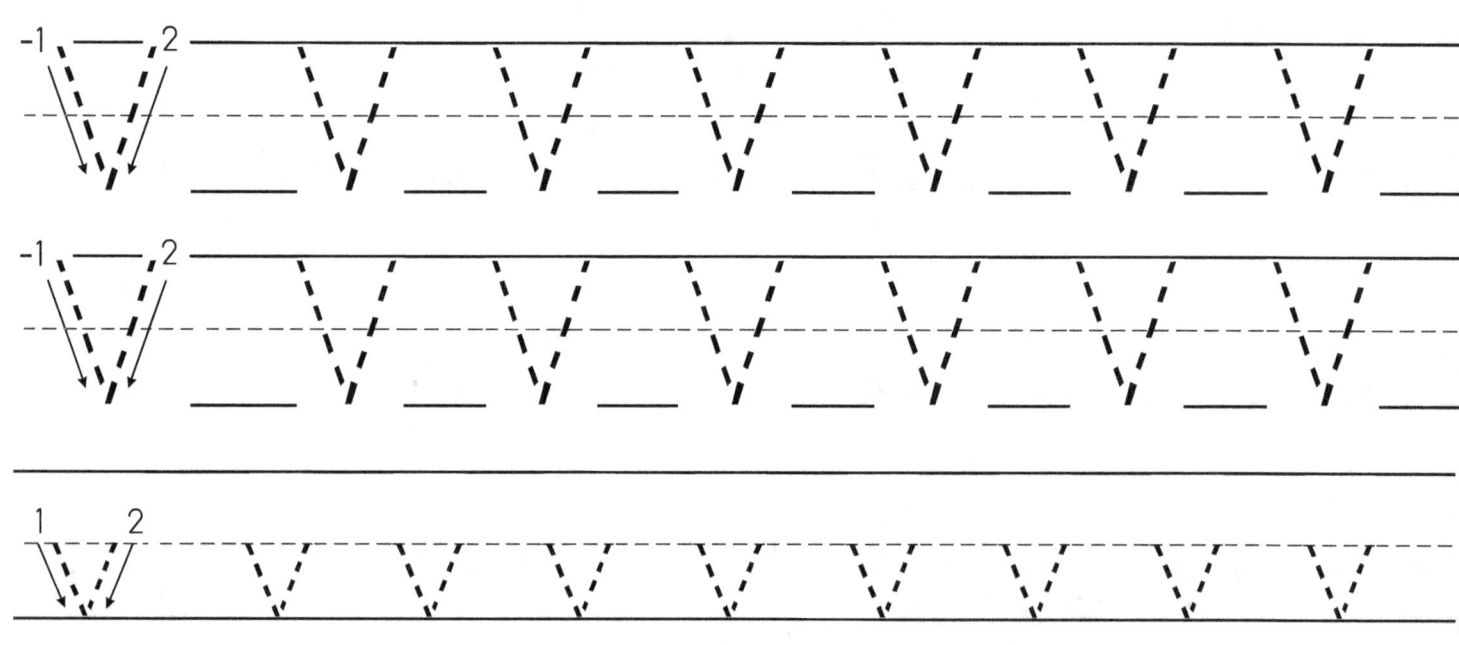

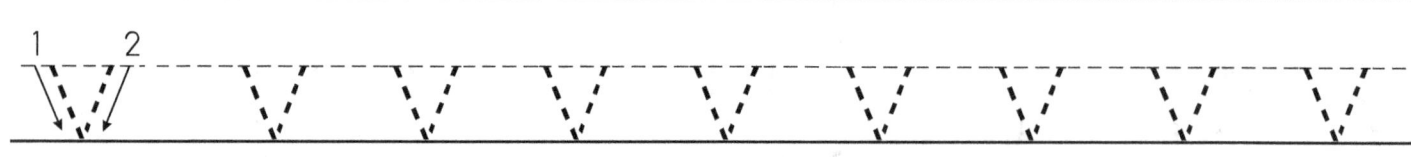

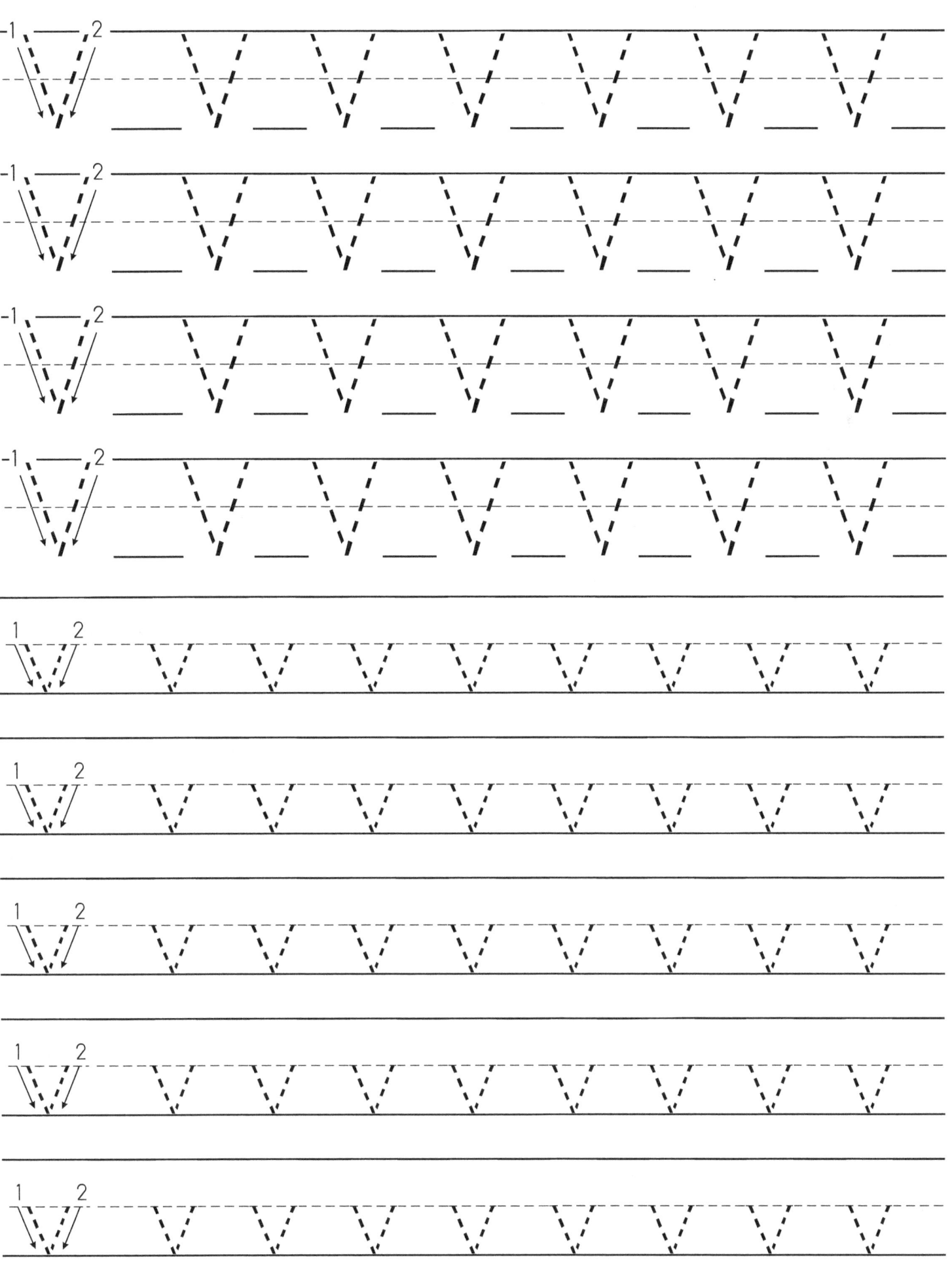

W Is For Watermelon

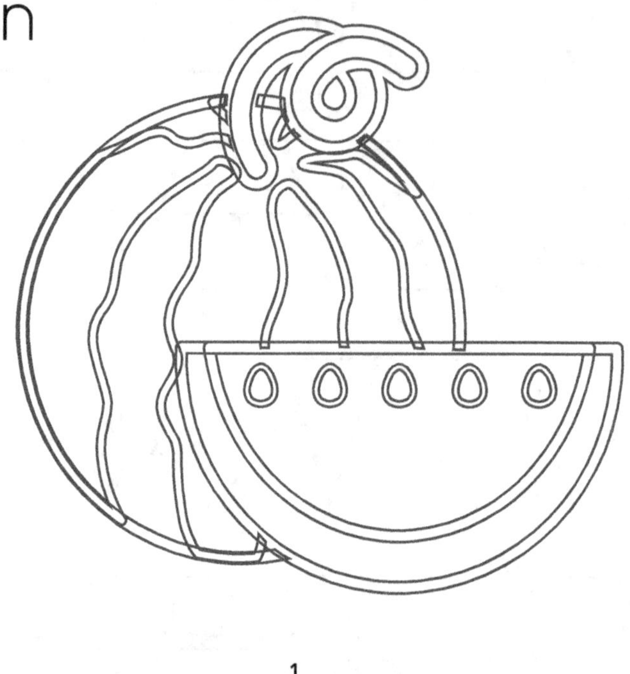

W w

watermelon

W W W W W W

W W W W W

w w w w w w w w w

w w w w w w w w w

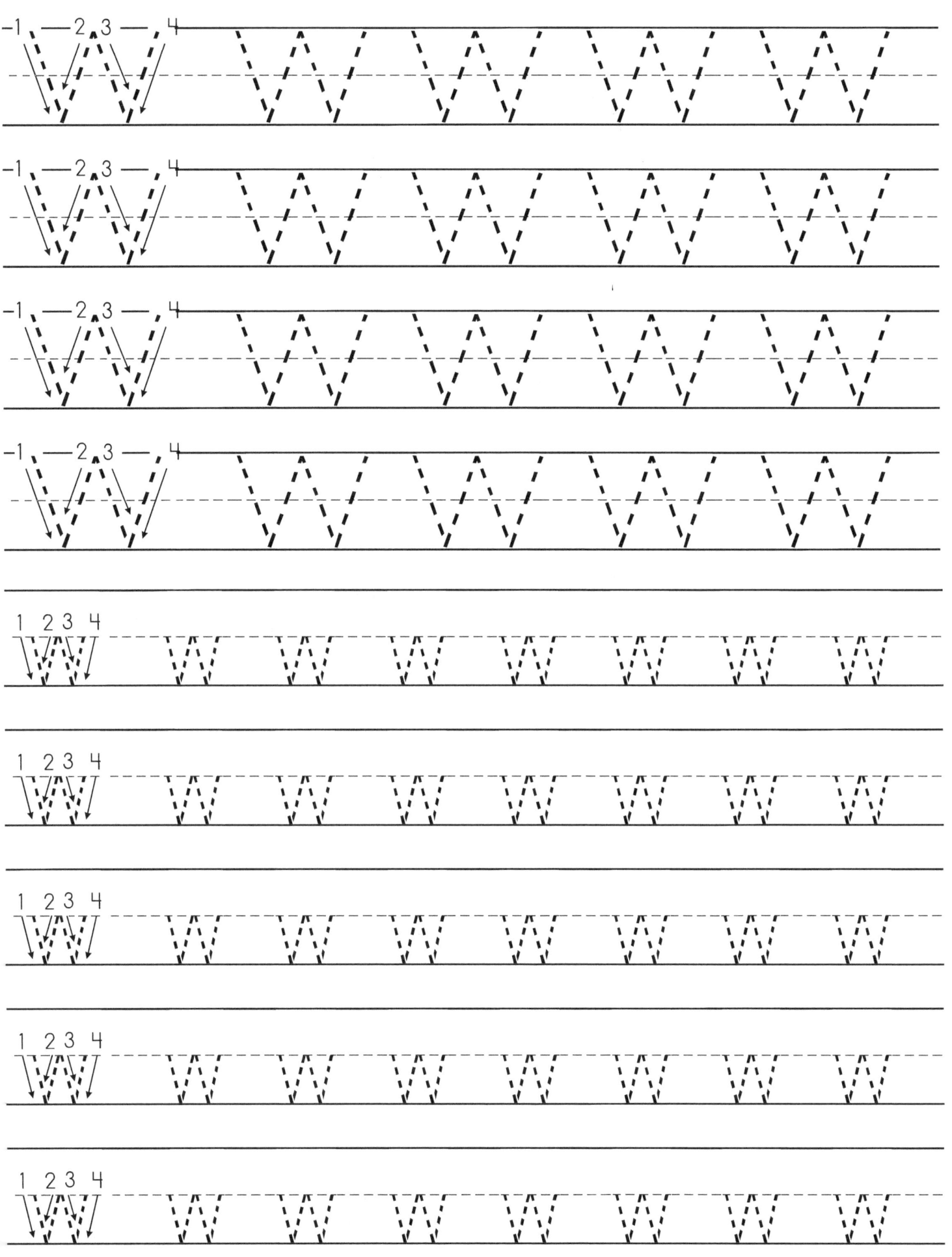

X Is For Xylophone

xylophone

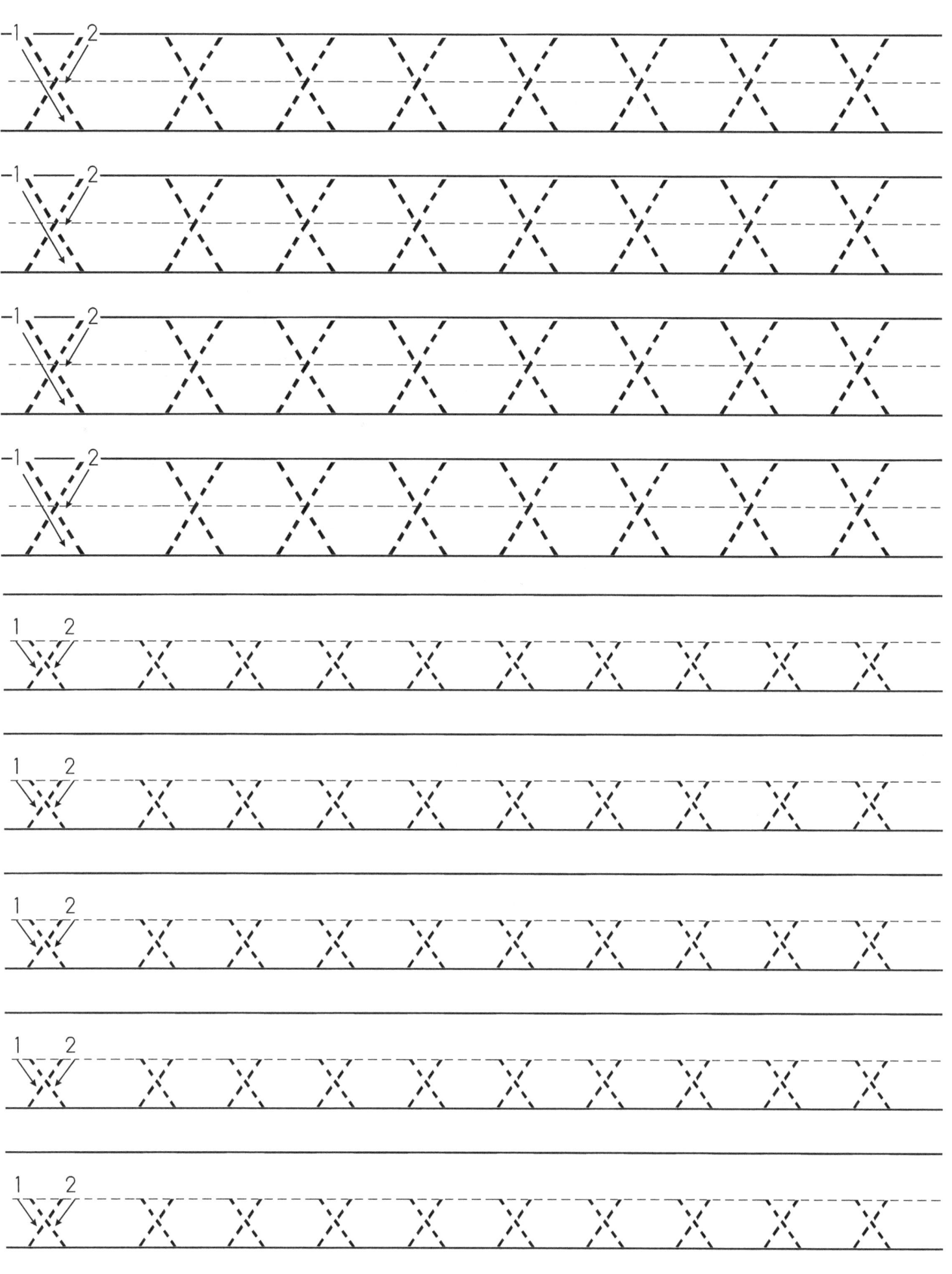

Y Is For Yacht

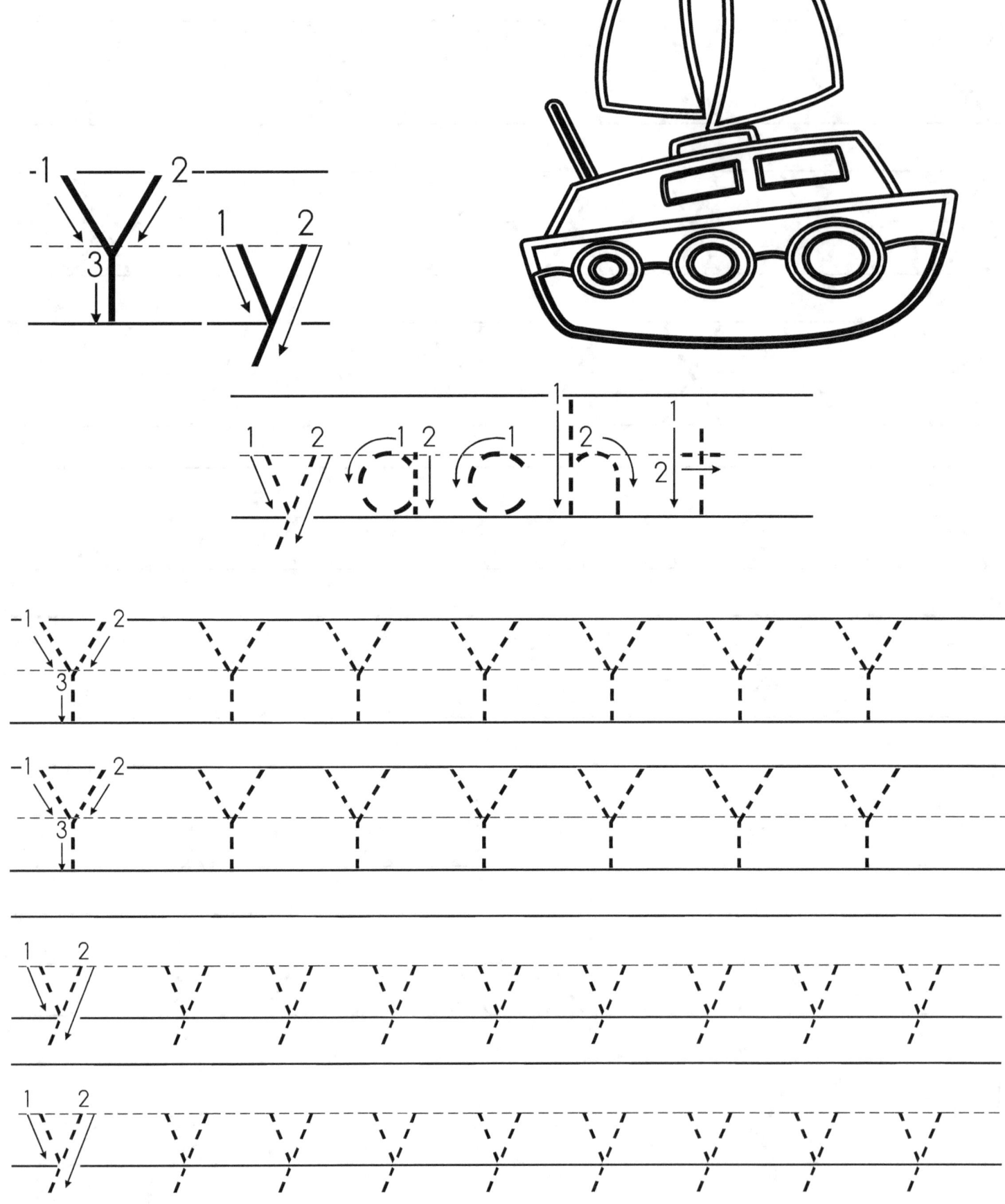

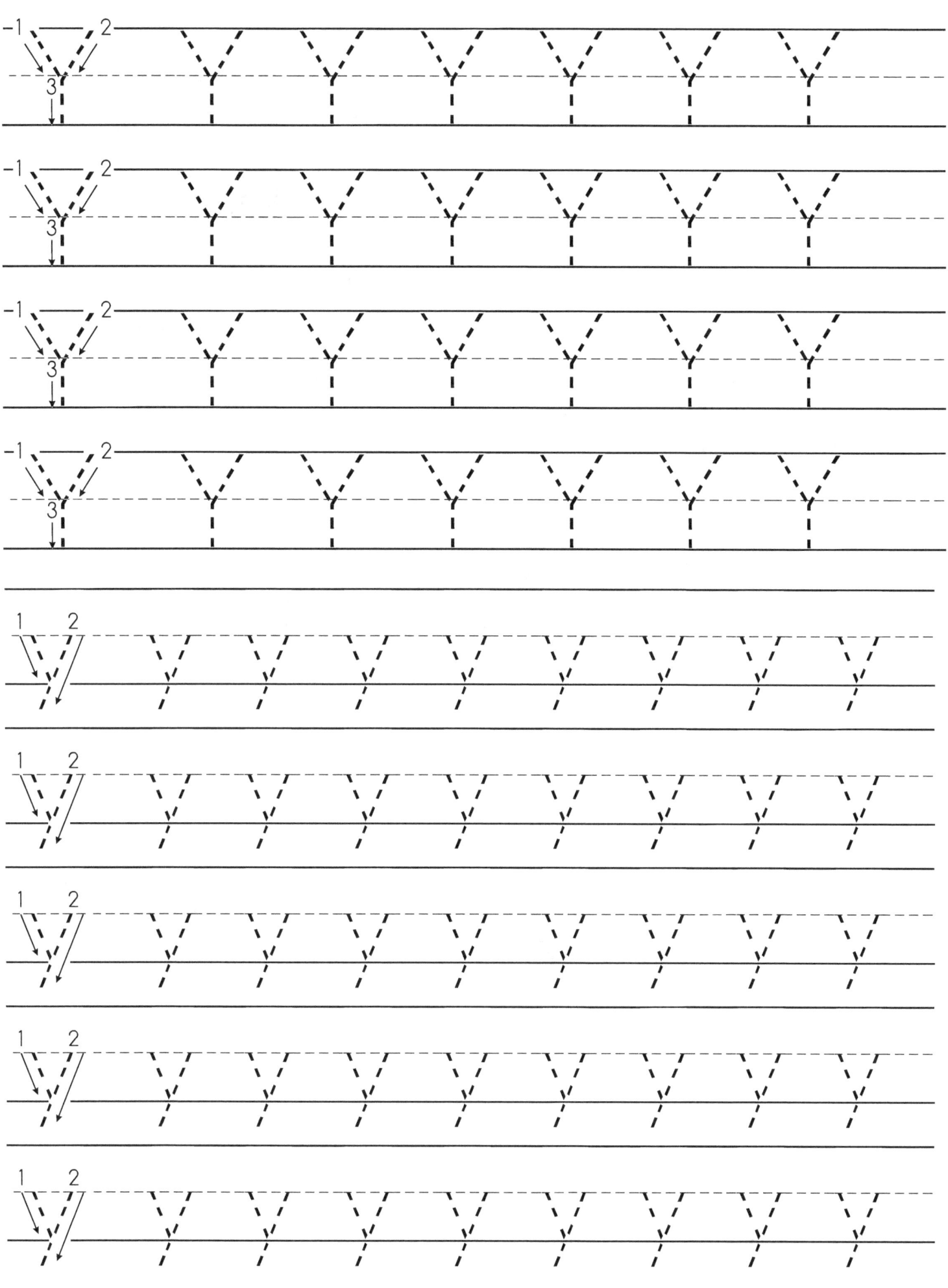

Z Is For Zipper

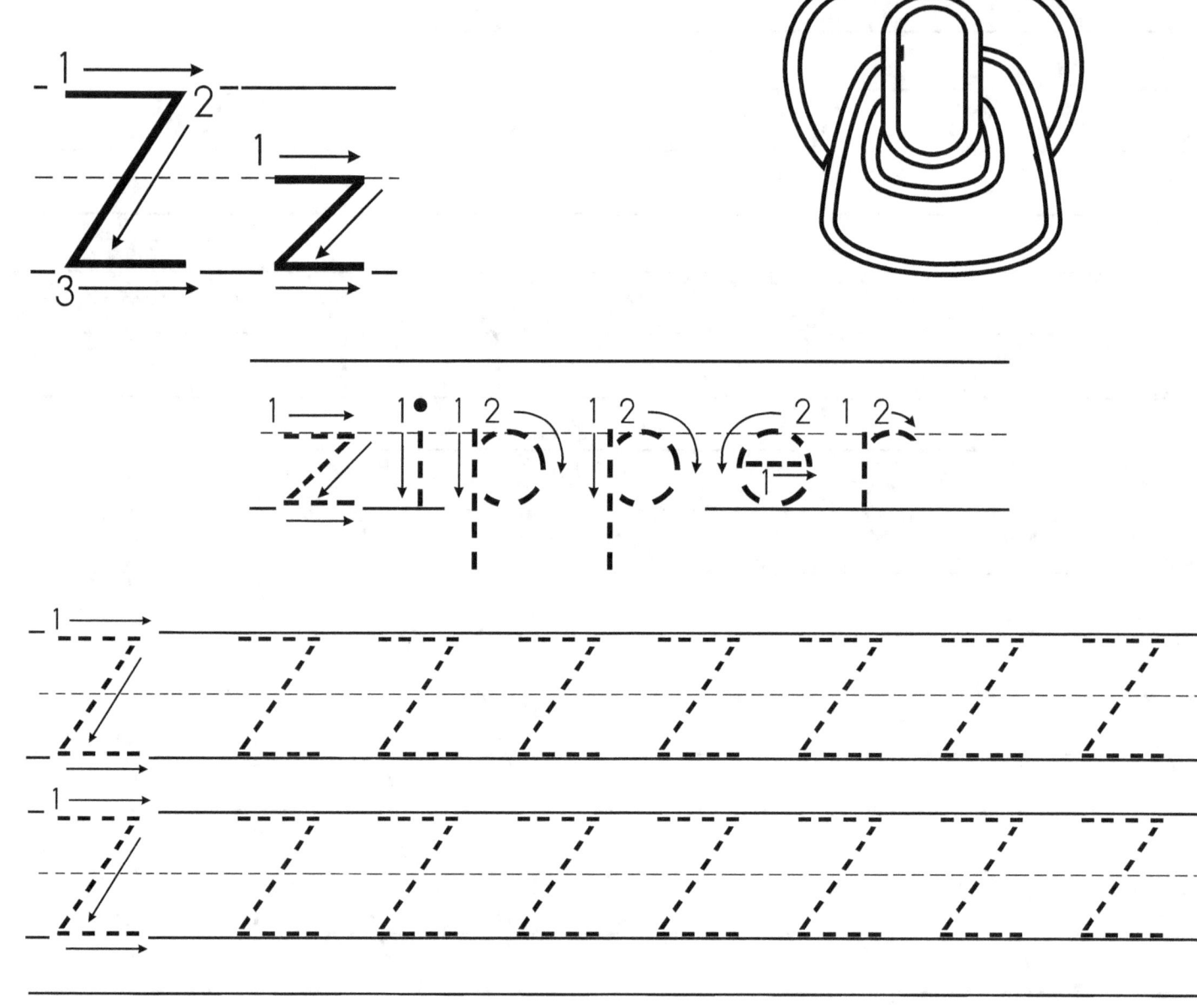

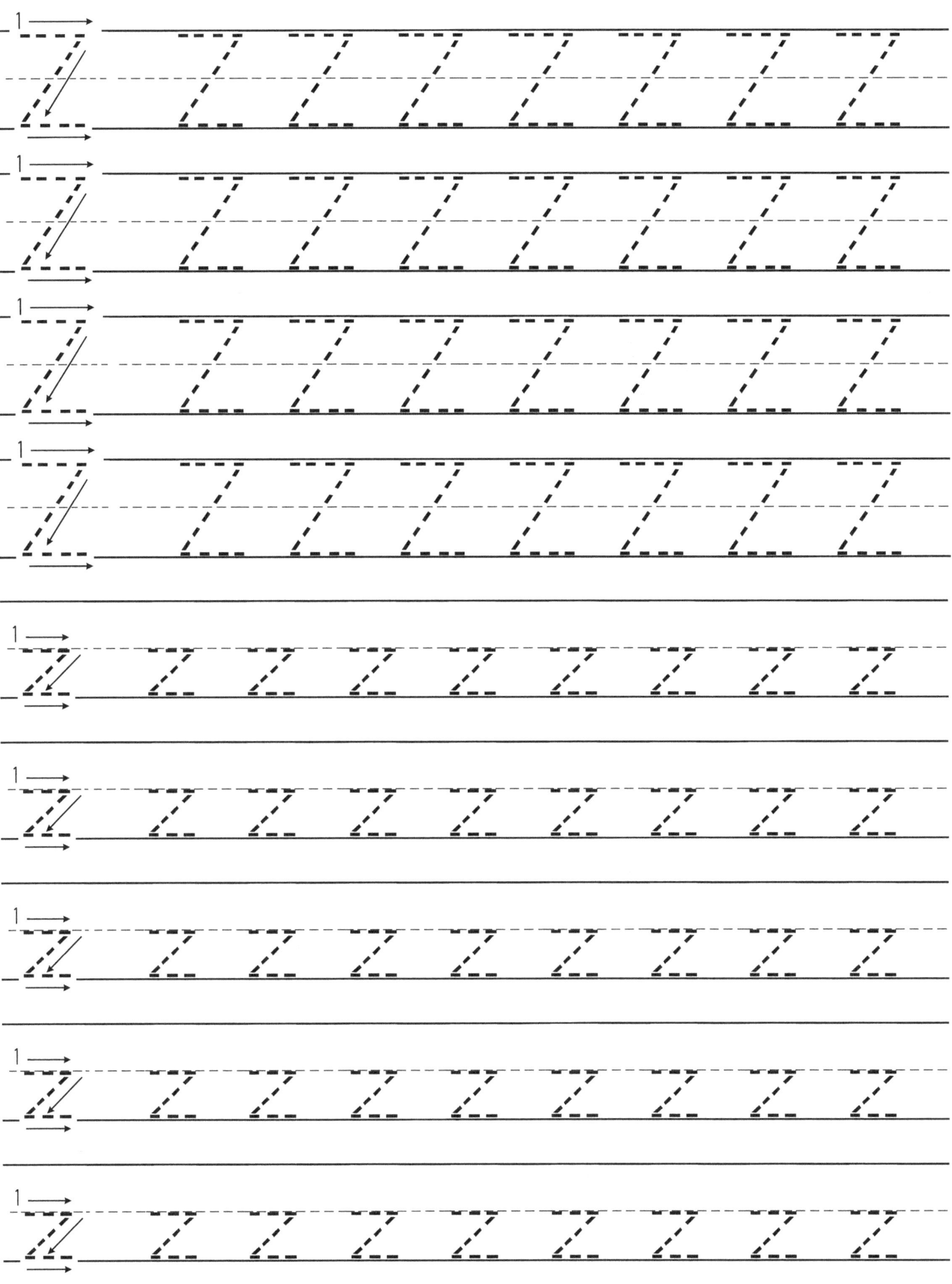